The Gifts of the Spirit by Dr. Verna [ ]
tation. Dr. Linzey shows how the spi. [ ]
history and how their biblical foundations, with practical applications, make them relevant to the twenty-first-century church. She
displays excellent theological and historical acumen, making this
book a must-read for any researcher on the topic. I highly recommend it.

—STANLEY M. HORTON, ThD
DISTINGUISHED PROFESSOR EMERITUS, ASSEMBLIES OF GOD
THEOLOGICAL SEMINARY

Verna Linzey writes from decades of experience and with a love for
the classical Pentecostal movement of which she has been a part all
her life. These are wise, heartfelt, and discerning words from a Pentecostal saint. They will be a blessing for all who desire the ongoing
manifestation of the presence of the Holy Spirit in their lives.

—AMOS YONG, PhD
DEAN, SCHOOL OF DIVINITY, REGENT UNIVERSITY
FORMERLY J. RODMAN WILLIAMS PROFESSOR OF THEOLOGY

Dr. Linzey clearly describes the role of the Holy Spirit in the life
of both the believer and the church. She places the work of the
Holy Spirit firmly within God's Trinity. By doing this, she brings
a refreshing approach on how God's grace is manifested in our lives.
When she explains the gifts of the Holy Spirit, she illustrates them,
giving biblical examples. At the same time she addresses problems
that have arisen with relation to the ministry of spiritual gifts. The
extensive bibliography she has included is a great additional asset.

—JEAN-DANIEL PLÜSS
CHAIRMAN, EUROPEAN PENTECOSTAL CHARISMATIC
RESEARCH ASSOCIATION

Verna Linzey is a true daughter of early twentieth century American Pentecostalism. *The Gifts of the Spirit*, her third book, follows her two previous well-received, award-winning works, *The Baptism With the Holy Spirit* and *Spirit Baptism*. This present contribution stands squarely in the trajectory of classical Pentecostal tradition by its emphasis on the person, work, and ministry of the Holy Spirit. Linzey's true impact will be found in the fresh clarity and balance that she offers this often-misunderstood subject. Linzey's work builds upon the foundation of the biblical text, followed by the offerings of the early church fathers, prior to launching out into contemporary worship experiences and applications. Her efforts are invaluable to seekers of a balanced pneumatology.

—Edward W. Watson, PhD
Professor of Biblical Literature and Practical Theology
Graduate College of Theology and Ministry
Oral Roberts University

Verna Linzey has given us a concise and insightful guide to the supernatural work of the Holy Spirit in the exercise of spiritual gifts. She speaks from years of study, wisdom, and practical experience. You will be as blessed as I was by reading this.

—Frank D. Macchia, ThD
Professor of Systematic Theology
Vanguard University of Southern California
Editor, *PNEUMA: The Journal of the Society of Pentecostal Studies*

The Gifts of the Spirit by Verna Linzey is written clearly. You will not need to consult a theological dictionary. Its language is easily understood and its scope comprehensive. All of the gifts listed in the Bible are covered. Each position Dr. Linzey proposes is based on Scripture. Thus the pages speak with compelling and uncommon authority. The book is encouraging. As you read, you will probably say to yourself, "I understand this. These gifts are intended for me today. I too can be blessed by the fullness of God's presence and power." Finally this book is empowering. A wise man once said, "The principal purpose in life is to keep our souls aloft." The principles Dr. Linzey advocates in this book are intended by God to keep our souls aloft. As Emily Dickinson wrote, "We never know how high we are until we are asked to rise. Then if we are true to plan, our statures touch the skies." This book encourages us to rise, to stay aloft, and to be true to God's plan, that our stature may touch the skies.

—David W. Plank, PhD
Translator, Modern English Version

The Gifts of the Spirit by Dr. Verna Linzey is theologically sound and historically accurate. This unique work empowers the church fathers to speak to today's church, explaining why the spiritual gifts are integral to a thriving, dynamic church. This vital resource is essential for every student and practitioner of the gifts.

—James F. Linzey, DD
Chief editor, Modern English Version

THE
GIFTS
OF THE
SPIRIT

THE
GIFTS
OF THE
SPIRIT

VERNA M. LINZEY, DD

CHARISMA
HOUSE

Most CHARISMA HOUSE BOOK GROUP products are available at special quantity discounts for bulk purchase for sales promotions, premiums, fund-raising, and educational needs. For details, write Charisma House Book Group, 600 Rinehart Road, Lake Mary, Florida 32746, or telephone (407) 333-0600.

THE GIFTS OF THE SPIRIT by Verna M. Linzey, DD
Published by Charisma House
Charisma Media/Charisma House Book Group
600 Rinehart Road
Lake Mary, Florida 32746
www.charismahouse.com

Cover design by Justin Evans

Visit the author's website at www.vernalinzey.com.

Library of Congress Cataloging-in-Publication Data
Linzey, Verna.
  The gifts of the spirit / by Dr. Verna Linzey. -- First edition.
      pages cm
  Includes bibliographical references.
  ISBN 978-1-62136-645-4 (trade paper) -- ISBN 978-1-62136-646-1 (e-book)
  1. Gifts, Spiritual. 2. Holy Spirit. I. Title.

  BT767.3.L56 2014
  234'.13--dc23

                                    2014026537

First edition

14 15 16 17 18 — 9 8 7 6 5 4 3 2 1
Printed in the United States of America

Contents

Acknowledgments... xiii

Foreword *by* Vinson Synan, PhD xv

Preface xvii

Introduction...xix

Chapter 1   Reflections From *a* Pentecostal "Saint"........................... 1

Chapter 2   Introduction *to the* Gifts *of the* Holy Spirit................4

Chapter 3   Historical Review *of the* Gifts *of the* Holy Spirit......10

Chapter 4   Scholarship *and the* Pentecostal Experience.............16

Chapter 5   The Church Fathers *and* Their Understanding *of the* Gifts *of the* Spirit 18

Chapter 6   The Person *of the* Holy Spirit....................................... 22

Chapter 7   Understanding *the* Godhead Before "Dividing *the* Persons" 27

Chapter 8   A Personal Relationship With *the* Holy Spirit 30

Chapter 9   The Holy Ghost *or the* Holy Spirit: Which Terminology Is Correct?... 34

Chapter 10   The Holy Spirit *and the* Counterfeit
                Supernatural..39

Chapter 11   The Moral Conviction *of the* Holy Spirit—
                the Hound *of* Heaven 44

Chapter 12   Why *the* Holy Spirit?.....................................47

Chapter 13   A Word *of* Wisdom.. 49

Chapter 14   A Word *of* Knowledge 55

Chapter 15   The Gift *of* Faith... 60

Chapter 16   The Gift *of* Healing..65

Chapter 17   Working *of* Miracles....................................... 70

Chapter 18   The Gift *of* Prophecy.......................................73

Chapter 19   Discerning *of* Spirits....................................... 82

Chapter 20   The Gift *of* Tongues 89

Chapter 21   Interpretation *of* Tongues.............................. 94

Chapter 22   The Seven Gifts *of* Romans 12...................... 98

Chapter 23   Wind, Fire, *and* Water—Important Metaphors
                of the Holy Spirit 102

                Notes.. 108

                Bibliography... 113

Acknowledgments

THE AUTHOR IS grateful to the following: Carla Bruce, who proofread the manuscript; Rev. Michael Pacella III, MA, MDiv, who provided assistance in the research and writing of the second draft; and Rev. Timothy B. Cremeens, PhD, who provided the bibliography from his unpublished work, *The History of the Charismatic Movement in the Orthodox Church in North America: 1972–1995.*

Foreword

ERNA LINZEY HAS accomplished many things in her lifetime. For over seventy years she has preached in many nations as an ordained minister in the Assemblies of God. Along the way she has been a musician and writer of hymns that are beloved by her Pentecostal friends. She has also published several books on Pentecostal themes, including her 2006 book *The Baptism With the Holy Spirit*. Now in her ninety-fifth year she has produced this new book, *The Gifts of the Spirit*.

With a long and distinguished ministry in the American Pentecostal movement, she is well qualified to write on this subject. She writes not only as a scholar, but also as a person who has personally exercised and manifested the gifts about which she writes.

This book is a valuable addition to the many books that have been written on the subject. Her first book introduced the reader to the Holy Spirit and His baptism with the initial evidence of speaking in tongues. This new book now introduces her readers to the long misunderstood gifts of the Holy Spirit, which are given to edify and strengthen Spirit-filled believers. This is a short and concise discussion of the gifts, which is sprinkled with classic hymns and prayers to the Holy Spirit that were handed down by holy men and women throughout church history.

At the end she also has included a very full bibliography, which should be useful to scholars and laymen alike. I recommend the book as a popular primer and introduction to the gifts of the Spirit and as a source for a deeper devotion to the third person of the Trinity.

—VINSON SYNAN, PHD
DEAN EMERITUS, REGENT UNIVERSITY
SCHOOL OF DIVINITY
SEPTEMBER 2013

Preface

WHY ANOTHER BOOK on the gifts of the Spirit? Many people have valid questions regarding the person and work of the Holy Spirit. This book addresses many concerns that, in my opinion, have not been satisfactorily answered. My prayer is that those who have been dissatisfied or confused by teaching on the Holy Spirit will not abandon the subject altogether but will continue to seek God for all He has provided for His people.

Experience with the Holy Spirit cannot be replicated. However, under the right circumstances, understanding of the person and work of the Holy Spirit can be gained. I have attempted to give a reasonable argument in this book to help the average person overcome the obstacles that hinder him from having a fuller relationship with the Holy Spirit. I hope I have been successful.

Carefully read each chapter so you will experience the full force of each argument. Reap the wisdom of the forbearers of grace by listening to rather than judging their experience with God. I believe that you will be enriched by considering the entire history of the work of the Holy Spirit, especially as presented in the New Testament. As the old adage goes, "The New is contained in the Old and the Old is explained in the New!" Imbibe deeply into the realm of the Holy Spirit, for God (the Holy Trinity) will lead the way!

—VERNA M. LINZEY, DD
ESCONDIDO, CALIFORNIA
SEPTEMBER 2013

Introduction

I HAVE ATTEMPTED TO write this book over many years, desiring to answer old questions in a more satisfying manner. Along the way I have consulted many Christian thinkers, both in books and in person, to make sure the issues I was addressing were of deep concern in the Christian community. Abuse is often associated with trying to bring clarity into a realm that has had dirt thrown into its clean, pristine water by those who have not fully understood the good intentions of the practitioners. May I apologize for those who in their lack of understanding may have given the wrong impression to those who were observing? God is very gracious and kind, so I hope my explanations will help to foster a spirit of cooperation among those with different expressions of their love for God.

Understanding is critical if we are to improve our dialogue as Christians. My prayer is that the lessons in this book will help readers connect the past with the present and thereby build a bridge of understanding. The implications are far-reaching, as we saw with the charismatic renewal that swept throughout the world and across denominational lines in the sixties and seventies. Organizations such as the Full Gospel Business Men's Fellowship International provided a platform for this move of God during those years. This helped build many bridges for Christians to cross in their attempt to gain a fuller understanding of one another and the ways of God.

This book examines traditional and historical aspects of the work of the Holy Spirit. Several problems are examined, and difficult passages are unpacked in an attempt to clarify common misunderstandings about this important subject. The work of the Holy Spirit is vast and is not limited to segmentation. The indivisible Godhead works in conjunction with all the persons of the Trinity to bring about the purpose and plan of God. This book will examine these mysteries in-depth while gleaning from the rich reservoir of classical literature. The Holy Spirit ultimately has one purpose, and that is to make the people of God holy.

A Word of Caution

Careful consideration and reverence are paramount in addressing an important topic such as the person of the Holy Spirit. There is no question but that the Holy Spirit continues to hover over the earth doing the work of God. However, not all actions done nor words spoken in the name of the Holy Spirit are truly from God's Spirit.

I do not intend to suggest that the aforementioned words and actions are demonic. Rather, they are more likely misdirected and purely human efforts credited to the Holy Spirit. Many corrections to misjudgments have ascertained that operations attributed to the person of the Holy Spirit were actually "works of the flesh." This is generally an innocent mistake made by believers who are new to the gifts of the Spirit or who have little teaching on the subject. Their intent is good, but the result is not.

For example, many "predictions" have fallen by the wayside; yet the credibility of the "prophets" who gave those wrong predictions was not diminished. I do not believe these people are evil or even false prophets. In my estimation, they are speaking out of their own hearts and not out of the heart of God. Therefore a word of caution is in order. Issues of misuse that have not been addressed as often or as thoroughly as they should have been in the past need to be examined. Grace is certainly needed in these situations when human frailty mixes with the perfection of God. This perspective also takes into consideration that humans are learning and may falter in the maturation process just as children falter when learning to walk.

Yet the fact remains that God's gifts are to be used to edify the "saints," not to manipulate them. Persons holding prophetic offices or having gifts of power must recognize that those gifts belong first to God. They do not belong to the individual; neither do they make the individual whom God uses to minster the gifts infallible or holy. A lack of discernment and clear distinction in this area has caused confusion in many gift-holders, and some have even developed a messianic complex, which has wreaked havoc in the sheepfold of God. Many examples of these occurrences are recorded in the history of Pentecostalism. However, to repeat a famous adage, we must not throw the baby out with the bathwater.

There are risks in seeking God and in experiencing the realm of the Spirit, just as there are risks in many other areas of life. For example, we risk the potential of death and injury when we get into a car or board an airplane. However, the reality that car and plane accidents can occur has not caused people to give up the benefits of owning an automobile or flying to faraway destinations. It would be wise to take a similar view when one is dealing with the use or study of the gifts of the Spirit.

Misuse of the gifts has brought ruin upon those ministering in an unscriptural manner as well as confusion and damage to innocent observers. This, however, does not mean we abandon the entire endeavor. Rather, we must proceed with caution and learn from our mistakes. This is why spiritual mentors and those who have tested the spirits over the years must be consulted and their wisdom embraced—which is one reason for the writing of this book.

Chapter 1

Reflections From *a* Pentecostal "Saint"

I T IS A great undertaking to reflect on a lifelong journey with God. Now in my ninety-fifth year, I feel compelled to relate my experiences and the lessons I have learned to the next generation. I attribute all of my success and reliability to the grace and mercy of the Lord Jesus Christ, for without Him, as the Scripture through the gracious lips of our Savior teaches, I can do nothing! The mystical journey the Lord has had me on is noteworthy. Many of my experiences coincide with those of believers across the ages. Jesus Christ is the same yesterday, today, and forever!

> The Lord God has given me the tongue of the learned, that I may know how to sustain him who is weary with a word; He awakens me morning by morning; He awakens my ear to listen as the learned.
>
> —ISAIAH 50:4

This text speaks about the importance of hearing and responding to the voice of God. The soundness of the faith is rooted in the sacred Scripture; however, the practice of the faith is in and through the work and person of the Holy Spirit. The person of the Holy Spirit not only gives us His gifts, but much like our Savior, He gives us of His very life force.

To set the tone for the nature of the book, I would like to relate a miraculous story that involves my late husband. During World War II, my husband, Captain Stanford E. Linzey Jr., CHC, USN, was stationed on the USS *Yorktown*. Saving Midway Island was a pivotal mission in winning the war on the Pacific front, and the *Yorktown* was one of the aircraft carriers (along with the USS *Enterprise* and USS *Hornet*) meant to ensure victory for the United States.

After the ship was hit with enemy fire, a sense of fatal despair filled the *Yorktown*, and Stan began to experience a tremendous fear of death. On June 3, 1942, Stan lay in his bunk praying in the dark, asking God to remove this fear. After some time in prayer God instantly removed the fear and gave him a deep sense of relief and peace. He no longer dreaded what would transpire in this battle.

I was in San Diego, California, which was about five thousand miles from Stan. I knew nothing of the attack on the *Yorktown* or Stan's experience in prayer. However, at this time I felt a strange need to pray in the Spirit, not knowing why. I knelt on the floor by the bed and prayed in the Spirit. It was between five and six o'clock in the evening. After about an hour I felt a release in my spirit and knew that God had answered my prayers.

When Stan and I later compared notes, we found that we had united in prayer that same day as we continued by faith to be sensitive to the moving of the Holy Spirit. Although the *Yorktown* was subsequently bombed and torpedoed at Midway, the battle was won and Stan survived.

One never knows when tragedy will strike our world, nation, or personal lives. Therefore we must be vigilant and pray in the Spirit on all occasions. Jesus said, "Peace I leave with you. My peace I give to you. Not as the world gives do I give to you. Let not your heart be troubled, neither let it be afraid" (John 14:27). Through praying in the Spirit, we may find ourselves in extraordinary leadership roles and contribute to the course of world events in positive ways. We must live by faith, be led by the Spirit, and lead by example. Then God will release His Spirit in us to help us be effective leaders in our spheres of influence in this world.

Chapter 2

Introduction *to the* Gifts *of the* Holy Spirit

W HY ANOTHER BOOK on the gifts of the Holy Spirit, you might ask? The truth is that there is more to say to bring needed clarification to the subject, as well as corrections that need to be made to prevent further misuse and abuse in the employ of these holy gifts.

In his description of the gifts of the Spirit for *The New International Dictionary of Pentecostal and Charismatic Movements*, noted Pentecostal theologian Walter J. Hollenweger, ThD, states:

> Just as music, normal speech, and the bread in the Eucharist are common gifts of creation and may be transformed in the liturgical context, so speaking in tongues and other gifts are natural gifts that many human beings may possess. Just as a cathedral is built of ordinary stones, so glossolalia and other gifts are ontologically natural and ordinary phenomena. And just as the stones in a cathedral do not change ontologically but functionally when put together in a masterpiece, so speaking in tongues and other gifts can become something like that, like the cathedral, proclaims, "God is here." This, however, is not the reigning understanding of the gifts of the

> Spirit in Pentecostalism and the charismatic movement.
> Usually they are understood to be strictly supernatural.[1]

While Dr. Hollenweger's view suggests a balance between the natural and the supernatural, there have been many faulty explanations of this supernatural phenomenon that in many ways deny the operation of the person of the Holy Spirit. True, there were many anointed craftsmen in the construction of the Tabernacle, but they were also endowed with supernatural ability by the Holy Spirit to perform with excellence to the glory of God. Bezaleel, of the tribe of Judah, and Aholiab, of the tribe of Dan, were two of the men the Bible explicitly says were filled with the Spirit of God and given special ability in workmanship to build the Old Testament Tabernacle (Exod. 31:1–11).

A song titled "Anointing Fall on Me" illustrates this concept. In it composer Donn Thomas stresses the importance of depending on the anointing of the Holy Spirit so that God's work can be done *by* God *through* human vessels. The song asks for God's anointing to fall and fill us—that every part of us would be touched by the power of the Holy Ghost. It does not appeal for an anointing on our natural ability but for the actual touch of God.

FACTS ABOUT THE GIFTS OF THE SPIRIT

The gifts of the Spirit are supernatural, and they "come upon" a believer suddenly in what is known as a "manifestation" of the Holy Spirit. They "flow through" a yielded, obedient servant of God. They have nothing to do with human ability, natural talent, or learned behavior. God never intended to accomplish the work of the church through human effort but through believers endowed with special spiritual qualifications whom the Spirit could direct and through whom He could work. The gifts are not "extras" or bonuses for those who are super-spiritual. They are essential operations in a properly functioning body of believers.

First Corinthians 12:4–11 lists the nine traditional gifts of the Spirit:

- Word of wisdom
- Words of knowledge
- Faith
- Gifts of healings
- Working of miracles
- Prophecy
- Discerning of spirits
- Different kinds of tongues
- Interpretation of tongues

To understand these gifts of the Spirit it is important to appreciate several facts about their nature, purpose, and operation.

The gifts of the Holy Spirit are not carefully planned actions or well-thought-out words.

Neither are they natural abilities to be used at a believer's discretion. The gifts of the Spirit are the divine tools or equipment God gives to believers so they will be effective witnesses for Christ. The gifts of the Spirit are "part of the package" believers receive when they are filled with the Holy Spirit. We could picture them as being in a toolbox the Holy Spirit hands us when we are filled with the Spirit (i.e., when we receive the baptism of the Holy Spirit). They are the "tools" that will get the job done as God intended. These gifts, like the tools in a toolbox, may require instruction as to their correct use, and those who are proficient in their use can help the beginner.

The gifts of the Spirit are not the same as the gift of the Holy Spirit.

Jesus gave the gift of the Holy Spirit to His followers after His death on the cross and His resurrection. When He had said this, He breathed on them and said to them, "Receive the Holy Spirit." (John 20:22). Then, just before He was taken up in a cloud and ascended to heaven, Jesus told His followers not to depart from Jerusalem but to wait for the Promise of the Father:

> But you shall be baptized with the Holy Spirit not many days from now.
>
> —Acts 1:5

> But you shall receive power when the Holy Spirit comes upon you. And you shall be My witnesses…
>
> —Acts 1:8

The gifts (tools) we receive are "power tools."

The gifts of the Spirit are the "shining forth" of Him who is within the believer.

Upon receiving the baptism of the Holy Spirit, believers have an anointing and power for the operation of the gifts of the Spirit in their lives. This anointing does not make one believer superior to others; neither does it mean one is more favored of God than another. When the gifts are manifested in a believer's life, that simply indicates that the believer is aware of the tools God has supplied and is willing to use them as God directs. The gifts of the Spirit are intended to draw attention to Jesus and lead the hearer in paths of righteousness. Never are they to exalt the one through whom the gifts are manifested. The gifts of the Spirit are not given for our pleasure or emotional enjoyment; however, when one is walking in the Spirit and being obedient to the leading of the Holy Spirit, there is pleasure and enjoyment. Never should we desire spiritual gifts for the thrill of the experience but for the honor of serving God and blessing others.

Spiritual gifts have specific purposes, as Scripture illustrates.

First, the gifts of the Spirit get the attention of the apathetic. Thus the display of the gifts may contribute to the salvation of those who previously had no interest in Jesus Christ. On the Day of Pentecost those gathered in the Upper Room began to speak with other tongues, which caught the attention of the multitude gathered in Jerusalem. After Peter preached to the attentive crowd, three thousand people became believers in Jesus Christ (Acts 2).

Second, the gifts convict people of their need for Christ. The word of wisdom, by which Jesus revealed the Samaritan woman's secrets, led her to salvation and to become a witness to those in her village (John 4).

Third, the gifts manifest the divine dynamic of supernatural power. The apostle Paul said that his preaching was not by persuasion through men's speech, but was a "demonstration of the Spirit and of power" (1 Cor. 2:4).

Fourth, the gifts give great glory to God. When Jesus healed the paralytic, the multitudes who witnessed this marveled and glorified God (Matt. 9:8).

The gifts are enhanced when subject to God's sovereignty, confirmed by character and conduct, and conformed to biblical truth.

First Corinthians 13, also known as the "love chapter," teaches that the absence of love nullifies the effectiveness of even the most powerful of the gifts; and the person trying to use the gifts without love is of no worth whatsoever. It is by design that Paul's teaching on love in 1 Corinthians 13 is bracketed between his teaching and emphasis on spiritual gifts. This reveals four important truths:

- ✦ The best gifts are no substitute for love.
- ✦ Neither is love a substitute for the gifts.
- ✦ The gifts flourish in an atmosphere of love.
- ✦ The gifts are expressions of love in action.

The gifts of the Spirit are desirable.

The gifts of the Spirit are desirable because of the One who gives them. They are love gifts given by Christ to His church. The gifts enrich, edify, and build up the one who exercises them, and they comfort, guide, reassure, confirm, bring healing, and provide God's rich blessings to those who receive them.

One's disposition works along with one's gifting. For example, consider John the Baptist. His development and disposition fit beautifully with the gifting of a prophet. The gifts and callings of God are a complete package. Samson, for instance, was not a ninety-eight-pound weakling; he possessed the physique of a warrior.

In later chapters I will deal with the many Scripture references to the gifts of the Spirit in an exegetical way. First, however, I want to establish the credibility of the gifts for the modern day and the appropriate manner in which they should be used for the edification of the church.

Chapter 3

Historical Review *of the* Gifts *of the* Holy Spirit

A REVIEW OF THE historical application of the gifts of the Holy Spirit is essential in order to evaluate the importance given to them for centuries. The classic handbook *A Manual of Prayers—Pontifical North American College* lists the seven gifts of the Holy Spirit as wisdom, understanding, counsel, fortitude, knowledge, piety, and fear of the Lord.[1] This list is evidently taken from Isaiah 11:1–2. This book also provides a list titled "Sins Against the Holy Spirit," which includes presumption of God's mercy, despair, impugning the known truth, envy at another's spiritual good, obstinacy in sin, and final impenitence.[2]

This volume also contains a prayer by St. Bonaventure (1217–1274) that makes an appeal for the seven gifts of the Spirit to "rest upon" the people of God:

> Lord Jesus, as God's Spirit came down and rested upon you, may the same Spirit rest upon us, bestowing his sevenfold gifts. First, grant us the gift of *understanding*, by which your precepts may enlighten our minds. Second, grant us *counsel*, by which we may follow in your footsteps on the path of righteousness. Third, grant us *courage*, by which we may ward off the Enemy's attacks. Fourth, grant us *knowledge*, by which we can distinguish good from evil. Fifth, grant us

piety, by which we may acquire compassionate hearts. Sixth, grant us *fear*, by which we may draw back from evil and submit to what is good. Seventh, grant us *wisdom*, that we may taste fully the life-giving sweetness of your love.[3]

This prayer/commentary gives us some insight into the understanding of the workings of the person of the Holy Spirit during the medieval era. As stated earlier, the list in St. Bonaventure's prayer is taken from Isaiah 11:1–2, which reads, "And there shall come forth a rod out of the stem of Jesse, and a Branch shall grow out of his roots. And the Spirit of the LORD shall rest upon him, the Spirit of wisdom and understanding, the Spirit of counsel and might, the Spirit of knowledge and of the fear of the LORD."

The workings of the person of the Holy Spirit should not be limited to gifts that manifest in an assembly of believers, however. Individuals whose sole purpose is to manifest the glory and nature of almighty God can also possess these gifts. It might be concluded that the church was not looking toward the New Testament assembly when it recorded the words of St. Bonaventure. Instead, it was looking at the Godhead manifesting God's nature through the people of God in character, not just in *charis*, or gifting. The Holy Spirit is present in this world to make the people of God holy—this truth should never be overlooked or minimized

The fruit of the Holy Spirit is a manifesting of the same person of the Godhead. The fruit of the Spirit listed in *A Manual of Prayers* is taken mostly from Galatians 5:22–23, but the list contains twelve fruit in contrast to the nine that typically are applied to His work in contemporary studies of the fruit of the Holy Spirit. Those twelve fruit of the Holy Spirit are:

+ Charity
+ Joy

- ✦ Peace
- ✦ Patience
- ✦ Kindness
- ✦ Goodness
- ✦ Perseverance
- ✦ Mildness
- ✦ Faith
- ✦ Modesty
- ✦ Continency (self-restraint)

Chastity[4] Another ancient prayer substantiates that what has been considered an all-encompassing list of the gifts and fruit of the Holy Spirit is incomplete. Great Pentecostal commentators such as Gordon Fee have pointed this out, especially in their works addressing these important issues. In Pentecostal circles there is a desire to pray for the presence and power of the Holy Spirit. This is nothing new. The ancients sought this act of grace; however, it was approached in a different way, as expressed through the following ancient prayer for the gifts of the Holy Spirit. It should be pointed out that in various studies the term *Holy Ghost* is rendered instead of Holy Spirit. The prayer reads:

> O Spirit of Wisdom, preside over all my thoughts, words and actions, from this hour until the moment of my death. Spirit of Understanding, enlighten and teach me. Spirit of Counsel, direct my inexperience. Spirit of Fortitude, strengthen my weakness. Spirit of Piety, make me fervent in good works. Heavenly Spirit, make me persevere in the service of God, and enable me to act on all occasions with goodness and kindness, charity and joy,

with long-suffering, mildness and fidelity. Let the heavenly virtues of modesty, continency, and chastity, adorn
the temple you have chosen for your abode. Spirit of
Holiness, by your all-powerful grace, preserve me from
the misfortune of sin. Amen.[5]

It is interesting that the prayer does not mention anything
about glossolalia but instead focuses on personal holiness because
the people of God are collectively and individually "temples of the
living God" (1 Cor. 6:19). Another prayer titled "Come, Holy Spirit"
or "*Veni, Sancte Spiritus,*" also has a different emphasis than the
Pentecostal church would propagate. It reads:

Come, Holy Spirit, fill the hearts of Your faithful and
enkindle in them the fire of Your love. Send forth Your
Spirit and they shall be created. And You shall renew the
face of the earth.[6]

The concepts of fire and renewal are present in the prayer; however, the emphasis is on love (i.e., the love of God is shed abroad
in our hearts by the Holy Spirit, as Romans 5:5 states) and not on
power and the manifestation of the Spirit. The prayer continues:

O God, who by the light of the Holy Spirit, did instruct
the hearts of the faithful, grant us in the same Spirit to be
truly wise and ever rejoice in His consolation. Through
Christ our Lord. Amen.[7]

I would like to close this chapter with another ancient prayer to
the Holy Spirit.

Creator Spirit all Divine,
>   come visit every soul of Thine.
And fill with Thy Celestial Flame
>   the hearts which Thou Thyself did frame.

O Gift of God, Thine is the Sweet
>   consoling name of Paraclete.
And spring of life, and fire of love,
>   and unction flowing from above.

The mystic seven-fold gifts are Thine,
>   finger of God's right hand divine.
The Father's Promise sent to teach,
>   the tongue a rich and heavenly speech.

Kindle with fire brought from above
>   each sense, and fill our hearts with love.
And grant our flesh so weak and frail,
>   the strength of Thine which cannot fail.

Drive far away our deadly foe,
>   and grant us Thy true peace to know,
So we, led by Thy Guidance still,
>   may safely pass through every ill.

To us, through Thee, the grace be shown,
>   to know the Father and the Son,
And Spirit of Them Both, may we
>   forever rest our faith in Thee.

To Father and Son be praises meet,
>   And to the Holy Paraclete.

And may Christ send us from above,
that Holy Spirit's gift of love. AMEN.[8]

Chapter 4

Scholarship *and the* Pentecostal Experience

TTEMPTING TO CAPTURE the Pentecostal experience in a scholarly work is like describing a love relationship with purely technical terms. Words seem inadequate to describe some experiences. I will attempt, however, to put substance onto structure, using persuasion rather than pure reason to substantiate my work. Faith is certainly reasonable; however, in this case faith is above reason while not defying reason.

Experience is very subjective, yet it has a basis from which it draws credibility. The early apostles interpreted their experience on the Day of Pentecost (Acts 2) by the insight and illumination they received from the person of the Holy Spirit. They attributed their experience to prophetic utterances in the Hebrew Scriptures (Joel 2). They learned to substantiate their external experiences by the parameters of the sacred Scriptures. Their use of the Septuagint, also known as *LXX*, was extremely helpful in establishing these parameters.

Experiences have an innate need to be clarified and deeply understood if they are going to direct the thinking and redirect the behavior of the recipient. Many strange and curious experiences have been recorded all over the landscape of Holy Scripture, and these have challenged scholars beyond their linguistic and historical insight. There is something about personal experience that shores up the credibility of theory.

I propose to share some of the experiences that have taken place within the sphere of the Pentecostal movement and prop them up with substantial theological reflection and exegesis. I will examine the thought of the "apostolic fathers," the "doctors of the church," as well as leading theological thinkers in both the ancient church and the church of the last two centuries. Special emphasis will be on those thinkers who have experienced the biblical experience of glossolalia. Exegesis (to draw out) and not eisegesis (to draw from) will be the method of inquiry applied to this important work.

Chapter 5

The Church Fathers'
Understanding *of the* Gifts *of the*
Holy Spirit

Ambrose of Milan (339–397), bishop and mentor to the great and celebrated thinker and theologian Augustine (354–430), completed a treatise on the Holy Spirit that is accessible for the modern reader.[1] The treatise is highly recommended for the contemporary reader who wants to understand the point of view of the early church on this important matter. There are many other comments on the ministry of the Holy Spirit by the church fathers dating as early as the first century. I will cite a few for your careful perusal:

Hermas (c. 150) wrote: "Crush not the Holy Spirit which dwells in you, lest he entreat God against you, and he withdraw from you."[2] It is very possible that Hermas was commenting on the dictum Paul the Apostle gave, which reads, "Do not quench the Spirit" (1 Thess. 5:19). This thought is expanded when Hermas says, "For if you be patient, the Holy Spirit that dwells in you will be pure. He will not be darkened by any evil spirit, but, dwelling in a broad region, he will rejoice and be glad.... But if any outburst of anger take place, immediately the Holy Spirit, who is tender, is straitened [constricted], not having a pure place, and He seeks to depart. For he is choked by the vile spirit."[3] This is an interesting exposition on grieving the Holy Spirit, and I believe it should behoove us to take heed.

Irenaeus (c. 115—c. 202), the bishop of Lyons, had much to say about the activity and person of the Holy Spirit. His exhortation should suffice in this context. It reads, "So now let us, receiving the Spirit, walk in newness of life, obeying God. Inasmuch, therefore, as without the Spirit of God we cannot be saved, the apostle exhorts us through faith and chaste conversation to preserve the Spirit of God."[4] To bring theological clarity to the person of the Holy Spirit, Irenaeus says, "The breath of life, which also rendered man an animated being, is one thing, and the vivifying [life-giving] Spirit is another."[5]

There are many more passages from fathers such as Tertullian (c. 155–c. 220),[6] Origen (c. 185–c. 253),[7] and Clement of Alexandria (150–c. 215).[8] Their writings should be examined for verification and continuity of theological thought.

The renewed emphasis on the manifestation and experience of the Holy Spirit requires theological reflection and must be in harmony with the Spirit's move in the past for authenticity. Even works by the great Jonathan Edwards record activity of the Holy Spirit that must be measured against the teaching and experience of the saints of old so that no accusation can be raised that the actions are not the work of God. Scripture articulates severe penalties for the grave error of not testing the spirits to ascertain if they are from God. The biblical parameters were given for our safety.

When dealing with the spiritual realm it is easy to succumb to deception if caution is not taken. Prudence is needed under these circumstances. Many casualties have been reported because people were careless when assessing their experience with the Holy Spirit. Many of the Christian mystics (i.e., mystical writers) have tried to explain how humans encounter the spiritual realm. Teresa of Ávila

(1515–1582) and John of the Cross (1542–1591) are positive examples of these types of mystical writers.

The person of the Holy Spirit, the third person of the Godhead, has been working in the world and over the face of the earth since the beginning. We must trace His fingerprint throughout history to discern His holy work. The works attributed to the person of the Holy Spirit cannot be rendered valid where they do not resonate with the historical record (Old and New Testaments) and with the "greater works than these" (John 14:12) done throughout church history. We cannot be ahistorical, meaning we cannot neglect the historical record of these events.

The church began at Pentecost, some two thousand years ago, not a hundred years ago when many Pentecostal experiences and teachings were rediscovered. This is important to understand since Jesus declared that He would build His church and that the gates of hell would not prevail against it. The church has not been destroyed from within, although at times she has suffered illness; the real danger is in separating her from her roots.

The work of the Holy Spirit has played a major role in bringing back to the collective memory of the church those important facts that keep her growing and pure. The Holy Spirit is teacher and comforter, reminding a forgetful church about her heritage so that she does not neglect so great a salvation. (See John 14:26.) Church history has much to teach about the current movement of the Holy Spirit. The misconception that the Holy Spirit ceased in His work until rather recently is absurd and uninformed; it is insulting to the powerful work that God has rendered throughout all known oral and recorded history.

I would like to close this section with a quote attributed to Origen:

The Gospel shows Him to be of such power and majesty, that it says the apostles could not yet receive those things which the Saviour wished to teach them until the advent of the Holy Spirit, who, pouring Himself into their souls, might enlighten them regarding the nature and faith of the Trinity.[7]

Chapter 6

The Person *of the* Holy Spirit

T ALKING ABOUT THE person of the Holy Spirit is a difficult task. After all, we are talking about a person of the Godhead. What an overwhelming undertaking! God has revealed Himself to humanity in many ways throughout recorded history. The greatest revelation to date has been the first Advent (the Incarnation), God assuming flesh in the person of Jesus Christ. The pouring out of the person of the Holy Spirit has been a great gift to the church. The fruit of the Holy Spirit in many ways reveal the nature and character of God throughout the world. This revelation is often manifested through the actions of people who are prompted by God.

In antiquity, the famous *Four Books of Sentences* by Peter Lombard (c. 1100–1160), provides the historical position on this doctrine so that we can keep it in context.

> For He is then said to be sent and/or given, when He is in such, that He makes us love God and neighbor, through which we remain in God and God in us. Whence (St.) Augustine, hinting at this manner of mission, in the fifteenth book *On the Trinity*, says: God the Holy Spirit, who proceeds out of God, when He has been given to men, enkindles him to love God and neighbor, and He Himself is love. For a man hast not, whence to love God, except from God…Nothing is more excellent [than]

that gift of God. It alone divides between the sons of the Kingdom and the sons of perdition. Other gifts are also given through the Spirit, but without charity they profit nothing. Therefore, unless the Holy Spirit be imparted to anyone, to make him a lover of God and neighbor, he is not transferred from the left hand (of Christ) to the right hand. Nor is the Holy Spirit properly said to be a gift except on account of the love, which the one who has not, even if he speaks every tongue, and has prophecy and every knowledge and every faith, and would distribute all his substance, and hand his body over, such that it burn, it profits him nothing. How great, therefore, a good it is, without which such great goods lead no one thoroughly to eternal life? But that very love and/or charity—for of the one thing is each name—leads thoroughly to the Kingdom.[1]

This book will attempt to keep in tension and in balance the motivation of love and the gifts of God manifested through God's people by the power of the Holy Spirit.

It must be emphasized that the Spirit of God is first holy and that God's mission is to make God's people holy by the ministry of the Holy Spirit in their lives. The warning by the apostle Peter to Simon Magus in the Book of Acts must be heeded today regarding the perception and the proper use of the gifts of the Holy Spirit. Some have treated the gifts disrespectfully, like power trips, and have disregarded the responsibility attached to exercising them. There is no room for showmanship or theatrics in administering these holy gifts.

The approach to this study will be to address each of the nine gifts separately, then to categorize them into clusters, illustrating their different functions. This approach will be unique because it will also consider the function of the gifts outside of the assembly or local church setting. Although these are not the only parameters that have been set up in the Holy Scriptures, holy tradition has instructed us that these gifts function wherever the saints (believers) are present. The Holy Spirit, as intimated previously, is a person and not a force. He is our helper, comforter, and teacher. I invite you to open your life to His ministry of love.

> There are varieties of gifts, but the same Spirit. There are varieties of service, but the same Lord. There are varieties of activity, but in all of them and in everyone the same God is active. In each of us the Spirit is seen to be at work for some useful purpose. One, through the Spirit, has the gift of wise speech, while another, by the power of the same Spirit, can put the deepest knowledge into words. Another, by the same Spirit, is granted faith; another, by the one Spirit, gifts of healing, and another miraculous powers; another has the gift of prophecy, and another the ability to distinguish true spirits from false; yet another has the gift of tongues of various kinds, and another the ability to interpret them. But all these gifts are the activity of one and the same Spirit, distributing them to each individual at will.
>
> —1 Corinthians 12:4–11, reb

These gifts are not natural endowments or talents; they are abilities infused by the power of the Holy Spirit. A person gifted with linguistics or translation is not necessarily dependent on the Holy Spirit for the operation of those gifts. We must make a clear distinction regarding the operation of natural gifts and supernatural dependence on the Holy Spirit. The infusion of the Spirit's power is supernatural and not due to our acumen or prowess in areas of competence. The gifts of the Spirit are not natural aptitudes; they are unearned "gifts" the recipient is to use for the common good. We are speaking of knowledge and wisdom that cannot be acquired through natural means. This was clearly illustrated in the life of the prophet Daniel:

> King Belshazzar gave a grand banquet for a thousand of his nobles and he was drinking wine in their presence. Under the influence of the wine, Belshazzar gave orders for the vessels of gold and silver which his father Nebuchadnezzar had taken from the temple at Jerusalem to be fetched, so that he and his nobles, along with his concubines and courtesans, might drink from them. So those vessels belonging to the house of God, the temple at Jerusalem, were brought, and the king, the nobles, and concubines and courtesans drank from them. They drank their wine and they praised their gods of gold, silver, bronze, iron, wood, and stone.
>
> Suddenly there appeared the fingers of a human hand writing on the plaster of the palace wall opposite the lamp, and the king saw the palm of the hand as it wrote. At this, the king turned pale; dismay filled his mind, the strength went from his legs, and his knees knocked together. He called in a loud voice for the exorcists, Chaldaeans, and diviners to be brought in; then, addressing Babylon's wise men, he said, 'Whoever reads this writing and tells me its interpretation shall be robed in purple and have a gold chain hung around his neck, and he shall rank third in the kingdom.' All the king's wise men came, but they could neither read the writing nor make known to the king its interpretation. Then

his deep dismay drove all color from King Belshazzar's cheeks, and his nobles were in a state of confusion.

Drawn by what the king and his nobles were saying, the queen entered the banqueting hall: 'Long live the king!' she said. 'Why this dismay, and why do you look so pale? There is a man in your kingdom who has the spirit of the holy gods in him; he was known in your father's time to possess clear insight and godlike wisdom, so that King Nebuchadnezzar, your father, appointed him chief of the magicians, exorcists, Chaldaeans, and diviners. This Daniel, whom the king named Belteshazzar, is known to have exceptional ability, with knowledge and insight, and the gift of interpreting dreams, explaining riddles, and unraveling problems; let him be summoned now and he will give the interpretation.

—Daniel 5:1–12, reb

Daniel clearly did not operate in his own skill or wisdom. It is in this sacred tradition that I introduce this study.

Chapter 7

Understanding *the* Godhead
Before "Dividing *the* Persons"

S CRIPTURE TELLS US that the person of the Holy Spirit, who is undivided, along with the Father and the Son, will lead the church into all truth. Chapters 14–16 of the Gospel of John are considered by some to be pivotal chapters on the person and work of the Holy Spirit. A quick review of those chapters will keep this truth in perspective. The Godhead has one "will," which gives expression to God's desire for His creation. The struggle of the will in the Garden of Gethsemane was the human will of Christ yielding to the spiritual will of God.

In relating to the person of the Holy Spirit, one must understand the complexity of the unity and the diversity of the Blessed Trinity. In relating to God, one does not establish a relationship with one person of the Trinity in neglect of another person, because God is one. The Lord Jesus in His earthly mission spoke of the person of the Holy Spirit but focused His attention on the Father, who historically is considered the font or fountainhead of the Holy Trinity. Because the complete work of the cross involved all the persons of the Trinity, humankind is able to enter into fellowship with the Godhead.

Therefore when we discuss the "gifts of the Spirit" we are talking about the graces of almighty God and not to the *charismata* exclusive to the person of the Holy Spirit—God is one. This understanding does not negate the distinctiveness of the persons; however, the three persons are all "God of God." The misrepresentation of the Father as being austere and the Son as being friendly—e.g., "You are My friends...." (John 15:14)—is a mischaracterization of the Godhead. All of the attributes of God are resident (in the form of mystery) in the Godhead united. The Holy Spirit is the exact representation of the Father and the Son, and the Son is the exact representation of the Father (Heb. 1:3).

A theology of the Holy Spirit cannot be separated from the Father and the Son. A theology that separates the persons of the Godhead does not understand the oneness of God's Being. At the baptism of the Son of God, Jesus Christ the Messiah, there was a theophany present illustrating the unity and the diversity of the Blessed Trinity. The Father spoke as in Creation, the Son manifested the Father's Word, and the Holy Spirit descended as a dove to bestow the anointing (Matt. 3:13–17).

The Holy Spirit is still present today, bestowing the grace and love of the Blessed Trinity on the sons and daughters of God. However, one cannot speak of the Godhead as if one could choose a favorite person, as if one could have a relationship with one person to a greater extent than with another. This practice has been prevalent in the United States since the Jesus movement in the early 1970s, during which the emphasis was almost solely on the person of Jesus Christ; in many circles today it still is! This misunderstanding of God could become heretical if it persisted.

As Christians we profess to be monotheistic. Historically though, Christians have been accused of being polytheistic due to the dividing of the persons of the Trinity, or tri-unity. Sending "the Counselor, the Holy Spirit, whom the Father will send in My name…" (John 14:26) is the work of God—Father, Son, and Holy Spirit.

Is it possible for the Godhead to split, to have differing opinions and wills? No! This idea is preposterous and should not even be entertained. Therefore when approaching the person of the Holy Spirit, beware of the heresy of modalism, which denies the distinctiveness of the persons of the Blessed Trinity yet calls God one in the sense of Me, Myself, and I. We are not saying that God is not three distinct persons; rather, we are saying that the unity cannot be broken or severed in any way. The closest that the Trinity has ever gotten to experiencing "division" was on the cross when Jesus cried, "My God, My God, why have You forsaken Me?" (Matt. 27:46). This agony of separation does not mean that the Lord Jesus Christ ever ceased to be God. It was similar in many ways to the experience at His baptism, where Christ fulfilled all righteousness, and later while in the tomb before descending into hell.

Chapter 8

A Personal Relationship With *the* Holy Spirit

T HERE IS A great deal of rhetoric today about having a personal relationship with Jesus Christ. This is both valid and theologically sound. However, because the Holy Trinity is indivisible, one cannot negate the fact that a personal relationship with Jesus includes a relationship with the heavenly Father and the third person of the Godhead—the Holy Spirit. We are instructed in Scripture to walk in cadence with the Holy Spirit, i.e., to walk in step with Him so as not to fulfill the lusts of the flesh (Gal. 5:16). To walk that closely with the person of the Holy Spirit, we must cultivate a relationship with the person of God "present" on earth—the Holy Spirit.

Jesus declared that He had to go back to the Father in order to send the Holy Spirit. This dynamic, though mysterious in light of God's omnipresence, is nevertheless an ontological reality. Being sensitive to the guidance of the Holy Spirit is an art of sorts. Grieving the work of the Holy Spirit can be detrimental to one's spiritual life. Therefore unless the believer cultivates a personal relationship with the Holy Spirit, the spiritual life of that believer will be hindered.

Walking with the Holy Spirit, as aforementioned, is an art. Man (generically speaking) is a free moral agent; however, a person can yield that freedom for the greater purpose of God to be realized on the earth. The Holy Spirit, as has been communicated over the centuries, is gentle and not pushy. If the fruit of the Spirit is love, joy, peace, longsuffering, gentleness, etc., I am convinced that God the Holy Spirit possesses these virtuous qualities and many, many more that would be difficult for the average human being to comprehend much less emulate.

I have heard a phrase that claims association breeds an impartation of sorts. The saying asserts that "there is impartation of virtue when there is association with virtuous persons"—at least that is the intimation. If a person does not formulate a personal relationship with the distinct person of the Holy Spirit, that person denies the words in the Nicene Creed, which (speaking of the person of the Holy Spirit) states, "With the Father and the Son together is worshipped and glorified."[1] The intimation is that the Holy Spirit should be worshipped and glorified.

The Holy Spirit has unique functions that distinguish Him in function but never in essence. He is our teacher, comforter, and friend. He provides guidance and gives insight and illumination to believers. He is a guide who is concerned with glorifying Jesus Christ as much as Christ Jesus was concerned about glorifying God the Father. This illustrates that all things in life should be done for the glory of God. The Lord Jesus in His earthly ministry could be present only in a limited way. The Holy Spirit, who has been "poured out" upon all believers, is accessible to believers on earth at all times. Consider the following prayer to the Holy Spirit:

> All Holy Spirit companion of the Father and the Son—
>   equal in essence,
> Thou Whom the Father and the Son love with an
>   eternal love,
> Grant that I may walk with You in peace.

> May I sense Your presence guiding me in life's way.
> May I yield to Your direction every day.
> Bond of the Father and Son—O heavenly Love,
> Grant me the fellowship of the Holy Thrice—
> God the Father, God the Son, and God the Holy Ghost.
> Amen.[2]

This prayer speaks of the essence of the Godhead and the functions that each person of the Godhead serves within this egalitarian relationship (i.e., in this shared love with humanity, which humanity has been invited to enjoy). In a desire to cultivate a relationship with the person of the Holy Spirit, one must understand who the Holy Spirit is through the revelation of Holy Scripture. One is confronted with the grandest reality of the Holy Spirit's function—to make others holy! Therefore unless one is interested in being made holy, a relationship with the Holy Spirit should not be pursued so directly; He is not interested in giving believers His gifts so they can have power. The power of the Spirit and the power gifts (e.g., miracles, healings, and discerning of spirits) are aspects of this relationship. However, a desire for power is not the priority. Pursuing a relationship with the Holy Spirit means desiring to be like Him—holy! The following prayers beautifully express that reality:

> Holy Spirit breathe on me—make me into Your holy
>   image.
> Communicate to me the language of the Godhead.
> Please bring me into Your sweet fellowship.
> Be pleased to mold me into a vessel of honor.
> Break me and heal me—so that I can be fit for Your
>   service.
> Pour forth Your love into the broken places of my soul.

And Grant me everlasting life—fellowship with You,
    The Father and the Son, forever.
Amen.[3]

Spirit of God All holy,
Participator in creation,
Re-create a clean heart in the recesses of my soul.
Grant me a burning love for the lost souls of the earth,
And forgive me for grieving your holy work in their
    precious lives.
Love me as the Father loves the Son and as the Son
    loves the Father and the Holy Spirit.
Make me into a vessel that can carry Your glory with
    dignity.
Be pleased to reside with me without interruption,
So that I may glorify Your name all the days of my life
    and throughout eternity.
Amen.[4]

Holy Spirit be pleased to reveal to me the mysteries of
    the Godhead.
Teach me how to hear, listen, and to obey Your gentle
    voice.
Illumine my heart in all of its darkness to understand
    the realm of the Spirit more fully.
I beseech Thee to keep me from deception in my pursuit
    of spiritual things.
Make a home in my heart for all eternity that will
    please the Godhead to dwell.
For Christ's sake.
Amen.[5]

Chapter 9

The Holy Ghost *or the* Holy Spirit: Which Terminology Is Correct?

I N RECENT THEOLOGICAL history a controversy of sorts has developed over proper terminology (Holy Spirit or Holy Ghost) when referring to the third person of the Holy Trinity. Perhaps this problem is simply semantics in the English language, or is it more than that?

As one reads ancient literature about the person of the Holy Spirit and pays close attention to how certain words are translated, this shift from "Holy Ghost" to "Holy Spirit" becomes obvious. In some circles the reason for this shift may be that history and the many ghost stories in our culture have contaminated the concept of a Spirit being holy. This is not the reason for the controversy in theological circles, where much is often made of little.

Is it superstition that is concerned with relating such a holy concept with such an apparently unholy one? This might be part of the problem, but it does not encompass the entire quandary. Would the concept of a Holy Ghost suggest that there is an unholy ghost? Would the concept of a Holy Spirit imply that an unholy spirit could be a rival? I covered many topics in *The Baptism With the Holy Spirit* (2005) and *Spirit Baptism* (2008), but I did not directly confront this apparently overlooked difficulty. Take for instance the 1662 version of the Nicene Creed in *The Book of Common Prayer*:

I believe in one God the Father Almighty,

Maker of heaven and earth,

And of all things visible and invisible;

And in one Lord Jesus Christ, the only-begotten Son of God,

Begotten of his Father before all worlds,

God of God, Light of Light,

Very God of very God,

Begotten, not made,

Being of one substance with the Father,

By whom all things were made;

Who for us men, and for our salvation came down from heaven,

And was incarnate by the Holy Ghost of the Virgin Mary,

And was made man,

And was crucified also for us under Pontius Pilate.

He suffered and was buried,

And the third day he rose again according to the Scriptures,

And ascended into heaven,

And sitteth on the right hand of the Father.

And he shall come again with glory to judge both the quick and the dead,

Whose kingdom shall have no end.

And I believe in the Holy Ghost,

The Lord and giver of life,

Who proceedeth from the Father and the Son,

Who with the Father and the Son together is wor-
shipped and glorified,
Who spake by the Prophets.
And I believe one Catholick and Apostolick Church.
I acknowledge one Baptism for the remission of sins.
And I look for the Resurrection of the dead,
And the life of the world to come. Amen.[1]

Compare this text to the 1975 ecumenical version from the
International Consultation on English Texts:

We believe in one God,
the Father, the Almighty,
maker of heaven and earth,
of all that is, seen and unseen.

We believe in one Lord, Jesus Christ,
the only Son of God,
eternally begotten of the Father,
God from God, Light from Light
true God from true God,
begotten, not made,
of one Being with the Father,
through him all things were made.
For us men and for our salvation,
he came down from heaven;
by the power of the Holy Spirit
he became incarnate from the Virgin Mary,
and was made man.
For our sake he was crucified under Pontius Pilate;
he suffered death and was buried.
On the third day he rose again

in accordance with the scriptures;
he ascended into Heaven
and is seated at the right hand of the Father.
He will come again in glory to judge the living and
the dead,
and his kingdom will have no end.

We believe in the Holy Spirit, the Lord, the giver of life,
who proceeds from the Father and the Son.[*]
With the Father and the Son he is worshipped and
glorified.
He has spoken through the prophets.
We believe in one holy catholic and apostolic church.
We acknowledge one baptism for the forgiveness of sins.
We look for the resurrection of the dead,
and the life of the world to come. Amen.[2]

What happened in the more than three hundred years of the creed regarding the use of the word *Spirit* over that of *Ghost*? Did popular literature force this shift? Consider the explanation offered by Scott P. Richert:

The *Holy Ghost* and the *Holy Spirit* are both historical names applied to the Third Person of the Holy Trinity. In English, *Holy Ghost* became the common title back in the seventeenth century, when the phrase was used in the two most prominent English translations of the Bible, the *Authorized Version* (*King James Bible*) and the *Douay Rheims*.

At the time, there was little difference between the

---

[*] This phrase is called the *filioque* clause (Latin for "and the Son"). Orthodox Christians profess the Creed without this clause.[3]

meanings of *ghost* and *spirit*. Today, the use of *ghost* to mean "spirit" or "soul" is considered archaic.[4]

This explanation may not be totally adequate. However, it may have to suffice to clarify that there really isn't a great difference in the understanding and meaning. So then, is it outdated to use this terminology in the twenty-first century? I do not believe so. Also, it is my belief that "Holy Ghost" should be restored so as to dispel the power that is given to the word in the realm of the evil one. There is one true Spirit in the universe—the Spirit of God. All counterfeits and those spirits that are in rebellion are not worthy to be compared with the one pure Holy Spirit (i.e., Holy Ghost), which is the person of God who is now present on earth.

> *Holy Ghost, lead us into all truth, so that we can glorify the Father and the Son as the glorious indivisible three in One.*

Chapter 10

The Holy Spirit *and the* Counterfeit Supernatural

PEOPLE IN GENERAL are enamored with the supernatural. Discernment to distinguish the difference between good and evil is essential so that people are not deceived. One of the deceptive schemes the enemy of our souls uses on the non-discerning is to appear to be an "angel of light" (2 Cor. 11:14). Both the Old and New Testaments contain accounts of counterfeit spirituality, which is spirituality not designed to glorify God.

Moses, in confronting the magicians of Pharaoh's house, engaged in a sort of competition regarding the credibility of each of the "sciences" being put forth as authentic (Exod. 7:8–13). When the apostle Paul was preaching the good news to an official, such a counterfeit person, a fortune-teller, readily took action against him in this same kind of showdown (Acts 13:4–12). If a person can "tell a fortune," that does not mean the person has a gift from God. Some people do not discern the source and sometimes attribute to that person a prophetic gift.

The devil has limited power in this realm but nonetheless has power. When Jesus was in the wilderness, the devil tried to seduce Him with lies and deception reinforced by his limited power (Matt. 4:1–11). Twice the devil misquoted and distorted Scripture, attempting to get Jesus to do something contradictory to God's Word. In the third temptation the devil showed Him (most likely in a vision) all the kingdoms of the world and said he would give them to Jesus if He would fall down and worship him. Jesus's response gives us the approach we are to take when faced with such temptations or when under such oppression. In each of the temptations Jesus responded with "It is written..." and quoted the appropriate scriptures that exposed the devil's deception.

In the book *Christian Theology: A Case Method Approach* coeditor Thomas D. Parker begins his theological introduction to the Holy Spirit with these words:

> The third article of the Creed professes faith in God the Spirit, "equal in power and dignity" to God the Father and God the Son. It lists the works of the Spirit which have to do with the salvation of humankind, viz. the Church, the communion of saints, forgiveness, the resurrection of the body, and eternal life. Some of the earlier versions of the Creed had merely the statement about the Holy Spirit, without any expansion, while the Nicene adds: the Lord and Giver of life, Who proceeds from the Father, Who is worshipped and glorified together with the Father and Son, Who spoke through the prophets...[1]

This theological framework is posited to establish the fact that the Holy Spirit is a person and not a force or some sort of power. The Holy Spirit is first holy and then deeply rooted in the personhood of the Godhead. Recognizing personhood is critical to understand in this theological framework. The orientation of the theologian in deliberating on the work of the Holy Spirit in the earth should be to see Him as a subject, not an object.

Power can become an intoxicating force, even in the life of the believer. When personhood becomes the issue, the focus can stay on the Godhead in its fullness.

Parker continues:

> In this form, the article represents the theological work of the Cappadocian Fathers, whose theological tracts on the Trinity gave attention to the third person as well as to the *homoousia* of the Father and Son and their relations...Their full trinitarianism gave the person and work of the Spirit its first consistent expression. Until the debates between Nicea and Constantinople, the Holy Spirit had not been a center for theological thought. Indeed, the simple trinitarian statement of the baptismal formula and the reality of the life and gifts of the Spirit had been the carrier of this element of belief, without any felt need for an expanded theological statement.[2]

The expression "Holy Ghost" has become out of vogue of late, due to the pagan connotations to the word *ghost* in modern vernacular. In Acts 13:4–12 one embarks upon a scenario that is quite unique even for the New Testament. Paul proceeds in an extremely confrontational way that could be perceived as combative. Luke communicates it in this fashion, according to Ronald Knox's 1944 translation:

> And they, sent on their way by the Holy Spirit, went down to Seleucia, and from there took ships for Cyprus. So they reached Salamis, where they preached God's word in the Jewish synagogues; they had John, too, to help them. And when they had been through the whole island to Paphos, they encountered there a magician who claimed to be a prophet, a Jew named Bar-Jesus. He was

in the company of the governor, Serius Paulus, a man of good sense, who had sent for Barnabas and Saul and asked if he could hear the word of God. And Elymas, the magician (that is what his name means when translated), opposed them, trying to turn the governor away from the faith. Then Saul, whose other name is Paul, filled with the Holy Spirit, fastened his eyes on him, and said; "Child of the devil, versed in all trickery and cunning, enemy of all honest dealing, wilt thou never have done with trying to twist the straight paths of the Lord? See, then, if the hand of the Lord does not fall upon thee now. Thou shalt become blind, and see the sun no more for a while." At this, a dark mist fell upon him, and he had to go about looking for someone to lead him by the hand. And now the governor, seeing what had happened, and overcome with awe at the Lord's teaching, learned to believe.

This account best illustrates the proposition rendered at the beginning of this chapter. Standing up to perversion and the contradicting of the truth is a great battle, especially against those who have acquired a counterfeit power. Moses and Aaron's encounter was no less dramatic although their victory was over a beast and metaphorically over the powers of the evil one. We read in Exodus 7:7–13 (according to Knox's 1948 translation):

Moses was eighty years old, and Aaron eighty-three, when they gave Pharaoh their message. And now the Lord said to Moses and Aaron. When Pharaoh asks you to show him signs of your mission, thou, Moses, shalt bid thy brother take up his staff and cast it in Pharaoh's presence; it will turn into a serpent. So Moses and Aaron gained Pharaoh's audience and did as the Lord had bidden them; Aaron brought out his staff in the presence of Pharaoh and his court, and it turned into a serpent. At this, Pharaoh summoned his diviners and magicians, who, in their turn, uttered secret spells in the Egyptian language and did the like; each man's staff, when he cast it down, turned into a serpent; but the staff of Aaron devoured them.

Just as this account illustrates, the counterfeit power of the devil always yields to the unflinching power of God.

Chapter 11

The Moral Conviction *of the* Holy Spirit—*the* Hound *of* Heaven

WHAT IS ONE'S conscience and what does it mean for it to be pricked? These tenable questions are alarming to some because they seem to presume the conscience is a viable entity. Whether the conscience is formed or unformed can be deliberated, but our purpose in this study is to consider what the work of the Holy Spirit is in this realm. Conviction, a word in ill-use in the twenty-first century, is the topic that must be examined.

Is guilt always bad, or does it have a positive effect? The book *Whatever Became of Sin?* by Karl Menninger, MD, addresses this subject. People are not persuaded by permissive counsel, which represses the tinge of conscience that most people experience when they sin. The Holy Spirit is convicting and convincing people of their sin every day, which is why people are surrendering their lives to Christ daily all around the globe.

A convicted man is not a condemned man. Condemnation results when one does not respond correctly to conviction. In the Book of Psalms King David expressed pain and other physical manifestations that resulted from this ignoring of conscience. (See Psalms 6; 38.) God is still at work in the earth, through God the Holy Spirit. He is working in the hearts of men and women in mysterious ways.

Insight is a word not normally attributed to the work of the Holy Spirit; however, this concept is very important to consider in this study. If one is seeing inside something that is not visible to the naked eye, then perhaps a spiritual dynamic is at work. Even if the specific insight is about a personal shortcoming or a way out of a secret sin, this may be the Holy Spirit at work.

Many so-called saints are in bondage to sin but do not want to recognize their serious spiritual disability. The Holy Spirit is at work to convince people, and to convict people, of actions and thoughts that are displeasing to God. The mystical and the intangible Spirit of God is always speaking to our hearts. One must tune in to the music the Holy Spirit is playing so that one can walk in harmony with His sweet and holy direction. This relationship with the Holy Spirit is a crucial part of the blending of hearts that creates sweet communion between the believer and God the Holy Spirit.

When in communion with the Holy Spirit, if believers begin to feel uncomfortable about their behavior they can be sure that the Holy Spirit is speaking. It has been said that God and believers (and unbelievers for that matter) are not compatible (because God is Divine and we are human) and that God does not change!

Sweet communion with the Holy Spirit comes when there is a clear conscience and an immediate repentance of one's sins. This on-the-spot repentance allows sweet fellowship to flow. Conviction from the Holy Spirit is not to make one feel perpetually guilty but to provide an opportunity for repentance and refreshing.

The Holy Spirit directs us and guides us, and that guidance intervenes into the realm of sin prevention. A spiritual alarm goes off provoking our consciences; in this way God the Holy Spirit helps us to avoid sin. When we are not sensitive to these warnings and indulge in sinful activities, there is still a way of escape. While we will reap the consequences of sin in the flesh, God has provided a way of escape in the spirit. "If we confess our sins, He is faithful and just to forgive us our sins and cleanse us from all unrighteousness"

(1 John 1:9). God does not want us to live under the torment of unconfessed sin; instead, He wants us to deal with it on the spot!

The conviction of the Holy Spirit will give us true direction for our lives—once we allow ourselves to be trained by it. The Spirit-led life that results from living with a clear conscience is sometimes hard to explain. However, the person who is walking in step with the Holy Spirit on a daily basis will be in tune to what I am trying to communicate for their benefit. I believe that some portion of the sin against the Holy Spirit has to do with the resistance to this kind of care.

Remembering that the gentle dove and the gentle dew describe some aspects of the ministry of the Holy Spirit (not in deference to the other revelations but in addition to them) helps one more fully understand this mystical relationship.

Chapter 12

Why *the* Holy Spirit?

WHEN ONE IS seeking the truth, it is important to know that one has a reliable guide. Sacred Scripture, endowed with the touch and inspiration of the Holy Spirit, has helped the church embrace all of God's truth. Jesus said the Holy Spirit will guide you into all truth (John 16:13). Without the guidance of the Holy Spirit, even spiritually mature believers are unable to discern the heights and depths of God's Word.

The spiritually dull seldom detect the work of the Holy Spirit because the realm of the Holy Spirit is in many ways intangible and the average person is more oriented to the material world. The vocabulary necessary to encounter the Holy Spirit's work is often out of the reach of the saint who is not always conversant with spiritual knowledge and the language that accompanies it. At this point, I am not speaking of the classical *glossolalia*,[1] better known as "speaking in unknown tongues."[2]

The Holy Spirit will often prompt, impress, or speak to the child of God in gentle, almost undetectable, ways. As the Christian becomes more accustomed to this type of communication, he or she will not miss these hints of guidance. The Holy Spirit also speaks in other creative ways; however, most of these experiences are subjective, and it would be irresponsible to codify them and to assume that everyone will have a common experience. Prodding believers toward personal holiness is one of the functions of the third person of the

Holy Trinity on earth. When God provides guidance, He does not push; instead, He leads us gently along the paths of righteousness.

Many forms of guidance, even spiritual guidance, can be deceptive. That is why the church is instructed to test the spirits to see if they are from God. John the Apostle learned this lesson firsthand through his impetuous desire to call down fire from heaven because of the inhospitable reception Christ and His message received in a certain Samaritan village.

> And when his disciples James and John saw this, they said, Lord, wilt thou that we command fire to come down from heaven, and consume them, even as Elias did?
>
> But he turned, and rebuked them, and said, Ye know not what manner of spirit ye are of.
>
> For the Son of man is not come to destroy men's lives, but to save them. And they went to another village.
>
> —LUKE 9:54–56, KJV

John shares the wisdom he gained from this experience—and one would be wise to heed his words:

> Beloved, believe not every spirit, but try the spirits whether they are of God: because many false prophets are gone out into the world.
>
> —1 JOHN 4:1, ALKV

Chapter 13

A Word *of* Wisdom

N SEEKING THE Holy Spirit, wisdom is supreme and should be acquired above all else. The acquisition of wisdom is a process that can take many years. However, in the realm of the Spirit it can be acquired instantaneously. One woman told of God directing her to give this word to a young youth pastor: "God will give you wisdom according to your faith, not your age."

The Holy Spirit gives wisdom to all who ask for it. Scripture says, "If any of you lacks wisdom, let him ask of God, who gives to all men liberally and without criticism, and it will be given to him" (James 1:5). James also juxtaposes wisdom from God with wisdom from below (from the devil) when he writes:

> Who is wise and understanding among you? Let him show his works by his good life in the meekness of wisdom. But if you have bitter envying and strife in your hearts, do not boast and do not lie against the truth. This wisdom descends not from above, but is earthly, unspiritual, and devilish. For where there is envying and strife, there is confusion and every evil work. But the wisdom that is from above is first pure, then peaceable, gentle, open to reason, full of mercy and good fruits, without partiality, and without hypocrisy.
>
> JAMES 3:13–17

This solid definition brings clarity and acuity to our under-standing of the wisdom of God in contrast to a false wisdom that has its origin in the evil schemes of the enemy.

However, the gift of a word of wisdom is part of a cluster of graces God provides for the building up of His kingdom. This is different from, and in addition to, the wisdom of God as described in the preceding paragraph. A word of wisdom often operates when one is faced with a difficult decision or when there are many options from which to choose. At times it can be puzzling for the believer who wants to please God in all things to decide on the proper course. A word of wisdom gives insight that was not resident until the Holy Spirit granted illumination. God provides this wisdom supernaturally.

One might ask how to know whether illumination and insight are from the Holy Spirit or from one's own mind. This concern will be discussed to provide practical and natural explanation regarding the working of the Spirit in the believer's life. (Note: the Holy Spirit and His operations are not a natural phenomenon; however, the workings of the Holy Spirit can be discerned by "[testing] the spirits to see whether they are from God," as 1 John 4:1 instructs.)

Those seeking God for wisdom often can find it in their own mouth or in the mouth of a close associate. Sometimes a word of wisdom works so naturally that one may not perceive its opera-tion. One needs to look at the nature of the manifestation to test its legitimacy. The Scriptures teach us something unique about the "wisdom from above," and provide criteria for our judging words of wisdom so we can decide whether to receive them.

It is important to establish that exercising the gifts of the Spirit without the fruit of the Spirit (character) can be destructive to the soul of the recipient. It is frightening to read portions of Scripture that invalidate the gifting of a group of individuals due to the misuse of the same (Matt. 7:21–23). Spiritual gifts should not be taken for granted or abused because, as the Scripture teaches, there shall be a day of reckoning. Just as a word of knowledge is not bestowed on someone who does not want to know, a word of wisdom is not imparted without the recipient seeking wisdom from God.

Let us distinguish between wisdom and knowledge to bring more clarity to the topic being considered. There are many levels and nuances to knowing a thing; to have wisdom with specificity causes one to be intentional when making decisions. God knows the future, and He knows the choices we should make. Rational calculation must be limited, however; spiritual insight is crucial for the decision to generate the favor and blessing of God. The Scriptures teach in the Book of Proverbs (which sometimes is called wisdom literature) that to be wise one must walk with the wise (Prov. 13:20). In so doing, wisdom is transmitted from one person to another. However, when a multitude of counselors is not present (a situation not unlike the one Nehemiah faced when he proposed a short, sudden exclamatory prayer to God in Nehemiah 2:1–8) where does one go? One must rely on the person of the Holy Spirit to provide the needed grace and insight.

What are some circumstances in which we might need wisdom? Perhaps choosing a lifetime partner or deciding whether to move to a different location. One needs the mind of God when making critical decisions such as these; and this wisdom can come only through the gifts and graces of God, imparted by the Holy Spirit.

As Jonathan shared gifts with David as a means of establishing their covenant (1 Sam. 18:1–5), so too has God given us gifts to equip us for the job of building up the church. Wisdom is a needed commodity in the life of the church. Opinions are usually free-flowing, but the wisdom that comes from above is not always discerned. A deep knowledge of Holy Scripture and an ability to interpret it soundly is critical when deciphering the truth. Even when we believe we have received a word of wisdom, we must still consult Scripture so we can be assured we are not running in vain, to echo the concerns of the apostle Paul (Gal. 2:2).

Wisdom is premium and must be diligently sought. Although the Scriptures are clear that prophecy is to be coveted and desired for the establishment of the church (the prophets and the apostles are foundational in the church), a word of wisdom for the local church or for the presbytery is desirable for times when there are many voices vying for the attention of the saints. I have witnessed many prophetic meetings in which egos were stroked and no wisdom was imparted. This has to change if the church is to mature. The sages of the past were sought out aggressively because people were being led astray like sheep without a shepherd.

A word of wisdom can sustain a weary one. The prophet Isaiah was able to declare this truth (Isa. 50:4) because he had disciplined his ear to hear from God. The constant cultivation of discipline and discernment will mature and prosper a person in the use of this gift. Wash your mind with the water of the Word so that your reservoir will be pure and not defiled by syncretism. Alloy and all impurities will defile this gift if it is not protected.

Wisdom is practical. It is instruction on what a person should *do*, not what he should *know* or meditate upon. Wisdom is directive; but, as was the case with the apostle Paul, who already knew what was going to happen to him in his future (in agreement with a prophetic word given by the New Testament prophet Agabus, as Acts 11:27–28 records), a word of wisdom can also be a source of confirmation (though it should never cause confusion).

FACTS ABOUT THE WORD OF WISDOM

This gift, like the word of knowledge and discerning of spirits, operates in the mental realm.

While similar to the word of knowledge, there are differences in the word of wisdom—none more important than the fact that God separately lists the two. We could say that wisdom is a correct application of knowledge or that it builds on material that knowledge supplies. A person might have many facts pertaining to a situation and in the natural see several possible courses of action. A word of wisdom will highlight the best possible course to take.

When speaking of wisdom, there are a few categories we need to consider:

- General wisdom—the ability to see what is right and do it.
- Personal guidance—when God gives specific, personal advice to His children through a word of wisdom.
- Anointed preaching—this comes through inspired preachers who share the words God has placed upon their hearts. This is essential in redemption and spiritual growth.

A word of wisdom is often effective in church government.

This is especially true when many opinions are being voiced. In Acts 6, when the disciples were murmuring about what to do concerning the daily administration of the church, the Holy Spirit gave them a solution. In Genesis Joseph had a word of wisdom when he was brought before Pharaoh. The apostle Paul gave many words of wisdom to the early church, especially at Corinth.

Wisdom for debate or defense also comes from the Holy Spirit.

Jesus said, "For I will give you a mouth and wisdom, which all your opponents will neither be able to refute nor resist" (Luke 21:15). Jesus also told His disciples not to worry about their defense when they were brought before rulers and authorities because "the Holy Spirit will teach you at that time what you should say" (Luke 12:12).

A word of wisdom is sometimes linked to personal revelation.

Paul's prayer in Ephesians 1:17 and Colossians 1:9 was that God would give "wisdom and spiritual understanding." James said that "the wisdom that is from above is first pure, then peaceable, gentle, open to reason, full of mercy and good fruits, without partiality, and without hypocrisy" (James 3:17). Only this gift is linked to qualities of good character. A word of wisdom will never be delivered in a controlling, bossy, or condemning manner. And the one to whom a word of wisdom is given would be far more likely to receive it when it is given in a gentle and peaceable manner. This gift is like its giver—meek and lowly in heart (Matt. 11:29). James speaks of "works by his good life in the meekness of wisdom" (James 3:13).

While both wisdom and knowledge are worthy of our pursuit, the gifts of the word of wisdom and the word of knowledge are more than an accumulation of wisdom or knowledge. God does not supernaturally pour out a great reservoir of wisdom on an individual from which He can draw any time He pleases. Instead, as the Spirit so wills, He gives a portion, a word, a fragment of that great storehouse of the Spirit. He gives just enough for the present situation. A word of wisdom will express the knowledge of God for a single moment—and that word will be sufficient for the occasion.

Chapter 14

A Word *of* Knowledge

K NOWLEDGE IS A glorious thing when accompanied by humility. Scripture is clear in its warning that knowledge makes one arrogant, or in the King James vernacular "puffeth up" (1 Cor. 8:1). Men and women seek knowledge because of an innate desire to know. This has been the collective wisdom of the philosophers, especially of Aristotle in his work on metaphysics. To know is to be informed about a certain subject; not to know is to be ignorant of said subject.

In discussing the gifts of the Holy Spirit as pertains to "a word of knowledge," we are not talking about inquiry, but rather reception. The prophet Jeremiah makes this dynamic clear when he says, as the "mouthpiece" of God, "Call unto me and I will show you great and mighty things that you never knew" (Jer. 33:3, author's paraphrase). The point when discussing a word of knowledge is that the Holy Spirit shares with the recipient knowledge that he or she never knew! I have seen this dynamic in action, and it can be very disconcerting for those to whom the words are being disclosed.

Unlike prophecy, a word of knowledge is not a forecast or prediction but a revelation of unknown knowledge shared by the Holy Spirit. The Lord Jesus Christ exhibited this gift in His first encounter with Nathaniel. He told him what he had been doing and where it took place. Another encounter during which Jesus used this gift was with the woman at the well in John chapter 4. He told her about her past and her current unmarried status, which revealed a lack of moral purity. This revelation astounded her to such a degree that she shared it as part of her testimony when relating her initial encounter with Jesus Christ, the God-Man.

A word from God can disentangle a tied-up life. A word from God can thrust a soul into his or her purpose on this earth. God knows our hearts, and when He reveals the secrets of our hearts to others it is an indication of how well He knows us. The Scriptures teach us that God knows us intimately—He knew us from our pre-born existence, and He knows the exact number of hairs on our heads. King David said that such knowledge was too wonderful for him; it was too high to attain (Ps. 139:6). God's knowledge of us is astounding. When God shares a portion of His knowledge in the form of a word of knowledge, He is declaring how very well He really knows us! This can be unsettling since God knows us better than we know ourselves.

One might ask, "Why would God reveal secret knowledge about an individual to someone who does not personally know him or her?" This is a good question and warrants an answer. God is omniscient, meaning He is all-knowing. Nothing passes unseen by His eyes, which are like a flame of fire (Rev. 1:14). God's knowledge purifies our hidden agendas; this is why God desires truth in the innermost parts of our hearts. (See Psalm 51.) God knows everything, and recognizing that He is omniscient puts the universe in perspective. At the judgment seat there will be no rationalizing because God already knows everything. We cannot inform God about anything because He already knows of its existence. When we are convinced that God truly knows us, we can more readily surrender to His awesome will.

Some scholars attribute the gifts of wisdom and knowledge to those who have acquired them through schooling. This approach is natural, but it does not take into account the working of the Holy Spirit, much like a natural explanation of the creation of the world disregards the Holy Spirit hovering over the universe and creating it along with the Father and the Son—the undivided Holy Trinity. Today's culture is so enamored with acquired knowledge that it has failed to discern true spiritual knowledge.

Jesus, the God-Man, acquired knowledge through maturation, as is evident from Luke 2:52, which reads, "And Jesus increased in wisdom and in stature and in favor with God and men." An explanation of this text would illuminate how He matured in wisdom and knowledge (one must have knowledge in order to apply it as wisdom), in physical stature (He was born a baby boy and matured to an adult man), in His relationship with God (He prayed regularly), and socially (His relationship with other people). This acquired knowledge is not the same as the Holy Spirit breathing on a given situation, thereby providing immediate insight concerning the matter. The word of knowledge can work very naturally and sometimes go undetected so that one might think he is a font of knowledge and insight when in reality it is the work of the Holy Spirit in his life. Knowledge that is acquired is important; however, it can never replace the disclosures of the Holy Spirit.

FACTS ABOUT THE WORD OF KNOWLEDGE

The word of knowledge declares an aspect of God's infinite knowledge.

God is omniscient—He knows all things. Therefore, at a time and place of His choosing, He can impart an appropriate piece of that knowledge to a believer. The word of knowledge will always be a word perfectly fitted to the situation and the person or assembly to whom it is delivered. Proverbs 25:11 could be describing the word of knowledge when it says, "A word fitly spoken is like apples of gold in settings of silver."

The word of knowledge is not carefully thought out and then spoken.

Rather, it is understood by the mind *after* the utterance is complete. All of the utterance gifts require complete trust in the One who imparts the word.

While we should always seek and study to increase in the knowledge of God, that is not the supernatural gift of the word of knowledge. The word of knowledge is one way God communicates to people through the inspired speech of a Spirit-filled believer. This "word" could also come via tongues and interpretation or through prophecy.

The Bible gives us many examples of this gift in operation:

- Jesus saw Nathaniel under the fig tree before he came to Him (John 1:48).

- Jesus knew Lazarus was dead without being told (John 11:14).

- Jesus knew the life story of the Samaritan woman (John 4:18).

- Peter knew the hypocrisy of Ananias (Acts 5:3).

- When the sailors wanted to abandon ship in the storm to save themselves, Paul knew that everyone had to remain on board in order for them to be spared (Acts 27:30–31).

- Elisha knew the location of the Syrian army and told the king of Israel (2 Kings 6:8–12).

- The disciple Ananias knew where Saul of Tarsus, who was then an enemy of believers, was staying and was sent to him by the Holy Spirit (Acts 9:11–16). At the same time Saul, who was blind at the time, received a vision of a man named Ananias coming to him and putting his hand on him so that he could see again.

+ Peter was told by the Holy Spirit that three men were at the gate inquiring for him (Acts 10:19–20).

The people to whom God gave these bits of knowledge did not know them naturally; the knowledge came supernaturally by the Holy Spirit. The knowledge was given to the individuals so that God's purposes might be accomplished.

Four kinds of knowledge are mentioned in the Bible:

1. General knowledge that we learn from books or experience.

2. Knowledge about God that is revealed in Scripture.

3. Knowledge of God based on a personal relationship through faith in Jesus.

4. The word of knowledge, which is supernaturally revealed to the believer through the Holy Spirit.

The word of knowledge is a fragment—a tiny bit—of God's knowledge given to us for a specific purpose.

It is the supernatural revelation of facts—past, present, or future—that cannot be learned through study or experience. The focus on this gift is not the *accumulation* of knowledge but the *transmission* of knowledge. It is knowledge miraculously conveyed—a divinely granted flash of revelation. The word of knowledge is not a faculty but a revelation. It is not an acquisition but a gift.

Chapter 15

The Gift *of* Faith[1]

F AITH IS BOTH a gift and a grace. While one might say "gift" and "grace" are similar in meaning, that would be only partially true. God grants all people the ability (faith) to believe, but this must be cultivated if it is going to grow. However, the gift of faith is a supernatural intervention allowing a person to believe extraordinary things—even for other people. As has been mentioned in the preceding chapters, there are times when certain clusters of gifts are given to certain people. This is especially true with gifts having to do with healings, miracles, and acts of compassion. However, the need for interdependence in the body of Christ provides an insight into how these gifts are dispersed abroad.

Does the gift of faith simply come on a person, or does this gift, like the gift and grace of teaching, have to be cultivated? This is an important question to consider and reflect upon, especially if we are going to receive a satisfying answer. As with the gift of teaching, God grants a certain level of aptitude; however, the perfection of that aptitude comes through use.

Faithfulness is an aspect of faith that has been downplayed in a culture that expects everything to come to fruition yesterday. A faith-filled person is a person of faith and is a faithful person. The person of faith grows in faith when his or her faith is exercised. King David confronted the lion, the bear, and then Goliath! It was a progression that enabled the young warrior to grow in his understanding of trusting God.

It is also interesting to note that at times the Savior chided the apostles for having such little faith. God requires faith (as little as a grain of mustard seed), yet the wavering of faith is unacceptable. The trust and the believing are in a *person*, not in a *formula*. Jesus said, "You believe in God. Believe also in Me" (John 14:1). What people believe and put their faith in reveals much about their character. If people believe in themselves, their government, or the stability of their company, they may falter. If they believe in God and in His unchanging character, as revealed through His Word, they are on solid ground.

We are called to be faithful, not faithless. However, there are times when we struggle to believe God's promises. Mark 9 tells the story of a man who was struggling with his faith. He declared— "Lord, I believe. Help my unbelief!" (v. 24). This is certainly not a case of the sin of unbelief, which we read about in the Book of Hebrews; rather, it is a genuine struggle with weak faith. With God's help we must overcome the unconverted areas of our hearts that resist believing by admitting when we are struggling with a lapse of faith. An old hymn declared that all things are possible if we only believe. How realistic is this exhortation? Is it truly that simple? I assert that there is more to a life of faith than just giving mental assent to a belief once. That is not the end of the journey.

FACTS ABOUT THE GIFT OF FAITH

The gift of faith is God's faith that "drops into our hearts" for a special purpose.

We are not talking about saving faith or the faith that increases as we grow in our Christian experience. The gift of faith is supernatural. God gives it to a person at a specific time and for a specific purpose. It is not planned or developed. The faith needed is just suddenly there.

One woman told of visiting a friend who had been diagnosed with cancer. The friend was believing God for healing, but this woman—as much as she would have liked—could not turn to her friend and say, "I believe you will be healed." As they sat in the living room talking about mutual interests, suddenly this woman felt the Holy Spirit rise up within her and she blurted out, "You're going to be OK!" Soon after that her friend's doctors declared her cancer-free.

Faith is the power with which God speaks and brings things to pass.

God said, "Let there be light," and there was light (Gen. 1:3). By the word of faith, Jesus turned the water into wine, multiplied the loaves and fishes, cast out devils, and raised the dead. The gift of faith is exercising the word derived from divine.

The gift of faith functions through men and women, yet it is the faith of God.

The gift of faith was operating when Peter and John healed the lame man at the Gate Beautiful. Peter said, "And His name, by faith in His name, has made this man strong, whom you see and know. And faith which comes through Him has given him perfect health in your presence" (Acts 3:16). One in whom this gift resides has close contact with God, receives His instructions, and allows the words and actions of faith to manifest.

The prophet Elijah had this gift. By faith he told the widow at Zarephath that her barrel of meal would not run out until the rain came—and it did not run out (1 Kings 17:8–16). The prophet Elisha also had this gift; he asked for the ditches to be filled with water, and they were (2 Kings 3:16–20). The apostle Paul had this gift. By the authority of the gift of faith Paul healed the lame man at Lystra (Acts 14:8–10).

The gift of faith differs from the gift of miracles.

This is true even though both produce results that transcend natural law. First Corinthians 12:9–10 lists the two gifts separately: "To another faith by the same Spirit…to another the working of miracles…" In some ways the gift of faith seems almost identical to the working of miracles. However, there are distinctions. The gift of miracles operates with immediacy, especially in actions that show forth God's greatness. Its effect on people, creatures, or things is generally objective. The parting of the Red Sea was a miracle (Exod. 14). The fig tree that Jesus caused to wither was an example of the power of faith. When the disciples were amazed at this phenomenon, He told them, "If you have faith and do not doubt, you will not only do what was done to the fig tree, but also, if you say to this mountain, 'Be removed, and be thrown into the sea,' it will be done" (Matt. 21:21).

A primary function of the gift of faith is to help the gifted believer.

This could be by supplying divine protection, physical provision, and assistance in one's work, among other things. While miracles often take place immediately, the outcome of faith may be deferred. Having to wait generally increases the gifted person's reliance upon God.

Neither mental assent nor human obedience is foundational to the gift of faith.

Rather, what is required is an unwavering trust in divine goodness and omnipotence (Heb. 11:27). This trust is so profound that trials cannot shake it. It is so absolute that it can survive even the loss of its own promised fulfilment, as we see in the story of Abraham and his son Isaac (vv. 17–19). By faith Abraham acquired Isaac, and by faith he was prepared to offer Isaac as a sacrifice.

God leads His people through progressive stages of faith.

Throughout this journey we must keep our eyes fixed on Jesus "the author and finisher of our faith" (Heb. 12:2).

The supernatural gift of faith is desperately needed in our time. It would give the spoken word a divine authority that none could resist, open up the resources of the kingdom of God to those in need, wither satanic opposition, and bring instant release from affliction.

Chapter 16

The Gift *of* Healing*

HE HEALING BALM of God's Holy Spirit is available to work in many spheres of a believer's life and must not be limited to healing in the body alone. One may be healed of an ear infection or a wounded heart; however, these graces are in a different category and require an insight that will clarify their distinction. The restoration of health to the body and the restoration of the believer's soul are equally important. King David cries out in Psalm 23, "He restores my soul" (v. 3). This restoration of soul includes every facet of the inner being.

God binds up the brokenhearted and then sets the captive free, as recorded by the prophet Isaiah (Isa. 61:1) and quoted by Jesus (Luke 4:18). This healing of the heart (which only God can do) is part of the healing ministry—it is healing on a deeper level. Many times inner healing, or regeneration of the soul, will even bring about physical healing, because in some cases physical sickness is related to spiritual sickness. (See James 5:15–16 for a fuller explanation of this important concept.)

Jesus performed many healing miracles during His earthly ministry. This alone did not establish Him as the Messiah or God; His deity manifested through His pure and sinless life—a life no other human being could replicate. However, healing was a significant

---

* There are times when this gift is referred to as the *gifts of healings* (plural), a theme that will be elaborated on in this chapter.

part of His evangelistic ministry. Many came to believe in Christ and in the gospel message through the ministry of healing. With that historical backdrop in view, let us examine the function of the healing ministry in the present day.

Many ministries in today's Christian landscape claim to see heal-ings and miracles on an almost daily basis. Most of these miracles are either witnessed during meetings, communicated through the media, or received by the formula of the confession of faith. While there are many legitimate experiences of healing, some are just a lot of hype. One must learn to distinguish between the reality of a hoped-for, but unrealized, healing and learning to bear one's cross.

Physical healing is a mystery in many ways. I have read of great healing evangelists who reported that skeptical unbelievers were healed when they came in from the streets to attend their meetings. Others who were believers and pleading for a healing (and many times justifying why they should receive the miracle) went away empty-handed! God is sovereign and people are not; therefore, we cannot demand anything from the hand of God even if we feel that blessing is part of our covenant rights.

We are God's creation, and God cares for us more than we can imagine; however, building character, not comfort (by way of healing) is sometimes the order of the day. The apostle Paul experi-enced some discomfort in his flesh (a "thorn" that continues to evade the insight of theologians) that God refused to remove. Instead, God provided the grace for the apostle to endure that thorn, what-ever it was. Much of the evangelistic ministry of the Son of God had to do with restoration, reconciliation, and healing the diseases of suffering people. The purpose of many of these healings was to bring salvation, not to keep creation perpetually untouched by sin and suffering. I once heard a comedian say, "I'm not going to die from anything serious!" Some believers approach the topic of sick-ness and healing with a similar mind-set.

Flesh and blood cannot enter the kingdom of heaven. The outer person is decaying, but the inner man is being renewed day by day. So what is the purpose of the ministry of healing? Is it just to draw the newcomer to salvation; or is it at the constant disposal of the believer, irrespective of how one conducts his life, because it is a benefit of the cross? Is everyone healed, and if not, why? I have lived over ninety years and have seen the mighty hand of God on my life and on the lives of others for whom I have prayed. However, are we to presume that healing always happens? I know from personal experience that some (demonically infiltrated) conditions do not yield except by much fasting and prayer. In some cases, even after prayer and fasting, an individual is not healed. Why does this occur?

Can a healing be lost or is it permanent? Is God required by the terms of the covenant to reinstate a person continually? From this context, is it to be understood that there will never be a good reason for one to die? Again the apostle Paul said that the outer man is decaying but that the inner man is being renewed day by day (2 Cor. 4:16). The New International Version renders it thus: "Therefore we do not lose heart. Though outwardly we are wasting away, yet inwardly we are being renewed day by day." Is this a true statement, or are we to expect to live forever in this fallen state? Oh, good Lord deliver us—and that He will!

The promise of healing and health does not mean that flesh and blood can inherit the kingdom of God; it simply means that God cares for His creation. Do people need the gift of healing? Absolutely! But they need wholeness more, a concept that includes the spiritual dimension of their beings. Healing is not limited to the physical body; it can encompass relationships, one's understanding—anything that can experience a breakdown. The Holy Spirit and His work are mysterious, as is evident by the inexplicable way He woos people to salvation. The same is true with the gift of healing, which can restore a broken heart and a broken jaw! However, sometimes the broken heart, which cannot be mended by a physician or a psychiatrist, must encounter the work of the Holy Spirit for true healing to occur.

It is important to note that though the gifts of healings (in the original text both *healings* and *gifts* are plural) may be clustered with the gifts of faith or miracles, these are all bestowed by the sovereign will of God, so there is not a predictable formula in their distribution.

Facts About the Gifts of Healings

Gifts of healings are divine enablements to heal the sick apart from natural means or human skill.

Yet while this is so, it is important to remember that God uses many means to accomplish His healing work. As previously noted, in the original text, both *healings* and *gifts* are plural. This indicates that this supernatural provision works in a variety of settings and situations. We want to be careful that we do not limit the expression of this powerful gift. Just as doctors and medical professionals use a variety of methods to heal, so the Holy Spirit uses a vast variety of methods to accomplish healing. The Scriptures give us examples: a word, a touch, laying on of hands, anointing with oil, prayer, and acts of obedience.

Sometimes the person ministering a gift of healing will tell the individual in need to do certain things; of course, this is always a Spirit-directed action. The prophet Elijah told Naaman the king to go and dip in the Jordan River seven times (2 Kings 5:10). Jesus told the man with the withered hand to stretch out his hand (Mark 3:5). Jesus told the man with palsy, who had been let down through the roof by his friends, to take up his bed and walk (Mark 2:4–11).

Other gifts of the Spirit are often used in conjunction with healing.

The gift of faith and the working of miracles are commonly evident in the ministry of healing. Consider, for example, when Jesus raised the widow's son from the dead. She brought her dead child to Jesus believing her son would be healed (Luke 7:11–15). In Matthew 9:20 a woman was healed when she touched the hem of Jesus's garment; Jesus told her it was her faith that made her whole. People were healed when Peter's shadow fell upon them (Acts 5:15). In Acts 19:11–12 we read that God worked unusual miracles by the hands of Paul, such that handkerchiefs or aprons from the apostle Paul were taken to the sick and diseases left. So we see miracles and healings combined.

Gifts of healings are action gifts that often produce signs and wonders.

Attention-getting signs such as healings were conspicuous in the preaching of the gospel in the early church. They revealed the love of Christ to a lost world. Our present generation would do well to seek the Lord earnestly for this seal of the Spirit upon our labors.

Chapter 17

Working *of* Miracles

THE WORKING OF miracles is in many ways similar to the gift of faith, since both produce results that transcend natural law. However, God's Word lists them separately. "To another faith by the same Spirit... To another the working of miracles" (1 Cor. 12:9–10). A careful study reveals that there are distinctions between the gift of miracles and the gift of faith. The gift of miracles operates with immediacy that show forth God's greatness. Its effect on people, creatures, or things is generally objective. The parting of the Red Sea was a miracle, for instance (Exod. 14:16). Additional examples are as follows:

+ Jesus turned water into wine (John 2:1–11).
+ The loaves and fishes miraculously multiplied to feed a multitude (John 6:5–14).
+ Lazarus was raised from the dead (John 12:17–18).
+ Philip performed miraculous signs in Samaria (Acts 8:5–6).
+ An angel told Philip to "go toward the south on the way that goes down from Jerusalem to Gaza." In obedience Philip started on his journey and met an Ethopoian man on the way. Philip told him the good news about Jesus, the man believed, and Philip baptized him. Philip then was miraculously

transported by the Spirit of the Lord to Azotus, where he continued preaching (Acts 8:26–40).

+ Peter miraculously escaped from prison when an angel appeared and the chains fell from Peter's wrists. Peter and the angel passed two guards without hindrance, and the iron gate of the prison opened for them by itself (Acts 12:1–10).

+ Paul and Silas were in prison when a violent earthquake occurred. Chains fell from all the prisoners, and the prison doors flew open (Acts 16:22–34).

FACTS ABOUT THE WORKING OF MIRACLES

Miracles transcend natural law.

Miracles occur through God's direct intervention—with or without human agency. The greatest miracle is the resurrection of Jesus by the sovereign act of God—no human being intervened or participated in order for that miracle to take place. Most other miracles recorded in Scripture involved human involvement, except the pillar of cloud that went before the Israelites in their wilderness journey. The parting of the Red Sea would be an example of a miracle that required human participation because God told Moses to stretch forth his rod in the direction of the sea. In another instance, the prophet Elisha made the axe float on the water at God's direct word. This miracle suspended natural law, but the prophet was a participant. The word *phenomenon* is often used when one cannot explain the occurrence. Some things truly are unexplainable. Human intelligence will never figure out the infinite purposes of our heavenly Father.

Jesus's ministry was confirmed by signs, wonders, and miracles.

Not only did Jesus perform miracles to relieve the suffering of the people and provide for them, but also He illustrated God's power to forgive sin with demonstrations of His power. Jesus asked people to believe on Him *because* of the works He did (John 14:11).

Miracles accompanied the preaching of New Testament evangelists.

These miracles were the credentials of those who claimed to be messengers of God. After the Day of Pentecost, the people of Jerusalem were amazed by the many wonders and signs the apostles performed (Acts 2:43). Miracles validated the ministries of Stephen, Philip, Paul, and Barnabas. The Book of Acts is filled with accounts of the miraculous displays of God's power.

Miracles and healings work to reinforce anointed utterance.

Simply put, miracles validate the preacher's claims (Rom. 15:18–19). Believers throughout the world have recorded the wondrous stories of God's unmistakable intervention in the course of ordinary human events. These stories have served to validate the gospel message and the truth of God's Word.

Chapter 18

The Gift *of* Prophecy

I S PROPHESYING SIMPLY forecasting, or is it also telling forth the word of God for the purpose of edification? Even in an eschatological context, prophecy is more than fortune-telling. The reason prophecy is distinguished from other vocal gifts such as tongues and words of wisdom is because of its power of edification. Building up the saints should always be the goal of those serving the Christian community. When there is a deep deposit of the Word of God in a community of believers, prophesying and edification will be the outcome. When the secrets of people's hearts are made known through the gift of prophecy, God is ultimately acknowledged and glorified.

Building up the church—not placating the saints—is the goal of true prophecies. A speaking forth or a telling forth of God's word is the purpose of the prophetic, not a predicting of the future. It is interesting to note that although there is an office of the prophet, even in the New Testament, all congregants are instructed that they may prophesy, so that all may learn, be comforted, and, most of all, be edified. (See 1 Corinthians 14:31.)

The gift of prophecy, in my estimation, is one of the most misunderstood and mishandled gifts. I have heard of charismatic leaders who claim that current-day prophecies are on par with those of the prophet Isaiah. This deception leads to a devaluing of the sacred Scripture.

Personal prophecies (which also have a precedent in the New Testament) in the current arena have at times been abused. Some people with the gift of prophecy have exalted the person being prophesied over and have made predictions that, in my estimation, are beyond their sphere of faith. This has caused people to put their trust in these "words from God," and in many cases it has directed their future path and pursuits. I was listening to one such "word" recently and realized that much of it had been conjured up by the speaker—none of it had come to pass. This gives authentic prophetic ministry a bad name. Testing the prophets and holding them accountable for their errors or misspeaks is critical if this gift is once again to serve its purpose of edifying the people of God.

Prophets can be dramatic, as was Agabus (Acts 11:27–30) when he prophesied that there would be a famine: "In these days prophets came down from Jerusalem to Antioch. One of them, named Agabus, stood up and prophesied by the Spirit that there would be a great famine throughout all the world, which came to pass in the days of Claudius Caesar. Then every disciple, according to his ability, determined to send relief to the brothers who lived in Judea. Indeed they did, and sent it to the elders by the hands of Barnabas and Saul."

In another instance Acts 21:7–14 gives us an example of personal prophecy communicated in a dramatic, Old Testament style reminiscent of Isaiah. Luke relates: "We finished the voyage from Tyre when we landed at Ptolemais, where we greeted the brothers and stayed with them for one day. The next day we who accompanied Paul departed, and arrived at Caesarea, and entered the house of Philip the evangelist, who was one of the seven, and stayed with him. He had four virgin daughters who prophesied" (vv. 7–9). It is interesting to note that while Philip's daughters prophesied, they were not counted among the prophets since the society was patriarchal.

Luke continues: "While we stayed there many days, a prophet named Agabus came down from Judea" (v. 10). Agabus then used

Paul's belt to illustrate the apostle's destiny: "When he had arrived, he took Paul's belt and bound his own hands and feet, saying, 'The Holy Spirit says, "In this manner the Jews at Jerusalem shall bind the man who owns this belt and deliver him into the hands of the Gentiles"'" (v. 11).

Let us look closely at these examples before we progress. First, Philip's daughters had the gift of prophecy, yet they did not share the knowledge that Agabus shared with the apostle Paul. Second, Paul is not dissuaded by this news! Luke records: "When we heard these things, both we and the residents [this would include the four unmarried women who prophesied][1] implored him not to go up to Jerusalem. Then Paul answered, 'What are you doing, weeping and breaking my heart? For I am ready not only to be imprisoned, but also to die in Jerusalem [this did not happen; he died many years later in Rome] for the name of the Lord Jesus.' When he would not be persuaded, we kept silent and said, 'Let the will of the Lord be done'" (vv. 12–14).

This example illustrates the distinction that was earlier mentioned—that all may prophesy. But this is poles apart from the office of the prophet. Agabus's sphere of prophecy was much broader than that of a believer who prophesies in the local church. The first prophecy cited was regarding a famine that came to pass. A false prophet does not have this kind of track record. This has been highlighted by recent predictions regarding the end of the world. Those "prophecies" did not come to pass—twice!

Yet the admonition recorded in 1 Thessalonians 5:20 must be heeded. In it believers are exhorted not to treat prophecies with contempt.[2] The fact that someone prophesies does not make him a prophet. This could be applied to preaching as well. Paul refers to himself twice as a preacher (1 Tim. 2:7; 2 Tim. 2:11). Peter calls Noah a "preacher of righteousness" (2 Pet. 2:5).[3] There are those who exhort and those who inspire, but that does not always translate into preaching. Charles Spurgeon was a preacher during the nineteenth century—the prince of preachers. It is with his example in mind that I distinguish between someone who speaks and a true preacher.

Facts About the Gift of Prophecy

The gifts of utterance (prophecy, tongues, interpretation of tongues, words of wisdom, and words of knowledge) all involve speaking. In Old Testament times prophecy was the sign that a person had received the fullness of God's Spirit. In the New Testament, after Pentecost, tongues became the evidence of the baptism with the Spirit. Thus we can say that utterance is a logical, spontaneous outflow and expression of the Spirit. Prophecy is the voice of the Holy Spirit. The gift of prophecy, then, allows God to use human voices who are yielded to Him to speak to His people.

The gift of prophecy is the only gift we are told to covet (1 Cor. 14:1, 39).

For this reason we must consider that it outranks the other gifts in importance. Other gifts often manifest through the gift of prophecy. For instance, prophecy is the voice through which wisdom speaks and the voice by which faith speaks.

To prophesy is to speak for another.

The one prophesying is speaking for God. Prophecy is also forthtelling as well as foretelling. To prophesy is to speak in one's own language in the power of the Holy Spirit.

The gift of prophecy is meant to edify (build up), exhort, and comfort (1 Cor. 14:3–4, 31).

One way to test a prophetic word to see if it is from the Holy Spirit is to determine if it falls within these three guidelines. A word of prophecy will never condemn, belittle, or tear down. The Holy Spirit uses the New Testament prophet as a voice to build up His church. Perhaps in some ways the New Testament prophet is much like John the Baptist—a voice crying in the wilderness.

The Holy Spirit does not bully a person to prophesy.

Rather, the Holy Spirit comes upon a prophet and encourages and inspires the servant of God to speak. Prophecy is an act of cooperation, where the one speaking cooperates with God. First Corinthians 14:32 says, "The spirits of the prophets are subject to the prophets." Prophets can control their own prophetic utterances—when and where it is appropriate to speak. For example, rather than interrupt a preacher in the midst of a sermon, it would be advisable to wait until after.

The gift of prophecy must be judged (1 Cor. 14:29).

One reason for this is that prophets can sometimes speak from their own hearts instead of from the Holy Spirit. It is possible for a prophet to add to the Holy Spirit's words or to give only part of the message. Sometimes the desire to encourage or comfort the one to whom he is speaking is so strong that it seems as though the words are coming from the heart of God. If a prophet is not certain that the message is from the Holy Spirit, it would be better to simply give a prayer of blessing. The apostle Paul warns, "Do not despise prophecies. Examine all things. Firmly hold onto what is good" (1 Thess. 5:20–21).

An important part of prophecy is to reveal divine truth.

However, the truth revealed in a prophetic utterance will never contradict the written Word of God (the Bible). Of course, some say we do not need prophecy today since we have the Bible; however, that position discounts how Bible truth coming to us through a spoken word of prophecy grabs our attention and penetrates deeply into our hearts. Experiencing the effects of this wonderful gift of the Spirit will make one a believer in prophecy. The twenty-first-century church needs the gift of prophecy as much as did the first-century church.

NOT DESPISING PROPHESYING AND ABUSE OF PROPHETIC WORDS

I link these subjects together because the abuse of the prophetic gift by some has indeed caused people to despise prophesying—or, if they do not hold prophecy in contempt, they want nothing to do with prophetic ministries. This is not a new problem since the apostle Paul wrote, "Do not despise prophecies," almost two thousand years ago. However, the charismatic renewal in the last half of the twentieth century not only revived the gift of prophecy in many mainline churches, but it also brought increased abuse of the prophetic gift. This may be because of a lack of teaching and experience in this area of ministry, which is why I believe my teaching on this subject is important for believers today.

Does every word given in the name of God qualify as an authentic prophetic word? Can prophetic words be used to manipulate a congregation? Do other prophets have a responsibility to judge whether a prophetic word is authentic? Is it right for some congregations to limit the gift of prophecy because of abuse or bad theology conveyed in some so-called prophecies?

Prophets must have a deep well of sacred Scripture at their disposal. The "Word of the Lord" must be deeply planted in their hearts and minds. True prophetic messages will never contradict the Scriptures. For example, Ephesians 2:8–9 says, "For by grace you have been saved through faith, and this is not of yourselves. It is the gift of God, not of works, so that no one should boast."

If someone gave a so-called prophetic word saying a person must belong to a specific church and give money to that church in order to be saved, that would be an obvious abuse of the prophetic gift. Other abuses might not be so obvious. Believers do not merely have the option to question whether a "word" is from the Lord—they have a biblical mandate to do so.

Any prophets who are erroneous on a continual basis should be asked to submit their "messages" to more mature and proven people who have been accurate in communicating this desirable gift. If they refuse to submit their insight, they should be prohibited from exercising their gift because their "prophetic" words could prove to be very detrimental to the flock.

Some people function almost like seers and appear to use the gift much like a fortune-teller. The recipients or hearers of this kind of a word need to exercise much caution and never act rashly on such a word. Seeking to know about the future can be dangerous, even when trying to predict events from the Book of Revelation (i.e., the apocalypse). I raise this issue because of a deep concern for the integrity of the gift that Scripture exalts above all other gifts. Any time the gift of prophecy is discredited, the church will suffer in the long run. Scriptural parameters must be followed in order for the prophetic word to be validated.

Jesus warned that many false prophets would come on the scene; yet our lack of discernment and our unwillingness to judge prophecies have caused much harm to the people of God. The issue of false prophets has not been adequately addressed in a contemporary setting.

People unwittingly submit to spectacular personalities who claim to have a word from God. Personal prophetic words can be even more deceptive. My understanding from those in the industry is that when bankers are learning how to detect counterfeit bills, they do not study the counterfeit currency but the genuine bills.

Likewise, a thorough study of the biblical gift of prophecy will enable one to identify a counterfeit use of the gift. It is helpful to be associated with an accountable group (a school of the prophets) that has a mechanism for bringing correction and adjustment for the safety of God's people. Submission to proven leaders is an absolute necessity for anyone ministering the gift of prophecy.

If you have ever been in a congregational meeting in which a prophetic word was challenged, you understand that this can be an embarrassing situation for the one prophesying. Prophets can sometimes be oversensitive because they feel as though they are guarding their "infallible" gift. No one but God is infallible! Many churches have bought into the belief that a prophetic word should never be challenged and corrected in the interest of the common good. Self-appointed prophets need to understand that they cannot function outside the government of the church. Scripture lists apostles then prophets in naming the fivefold ministry gifts (Eph. 4:11).

A church will be out of balance if it is governed by a prophetic voice and not by primary apostolic authority. Consider, for example, if an apostolic leader gives a message then a prophetic voice comes to modify or even oppose or contradict it. How should this situation be handled? The apostolic is like the king and the prophetic is subject to the king's authority (you might cite Nathan the prophet confronting David the king and miss the point of this inquiry). The apostolic leader is like the king who has the rule. The prophetic is there to undergird, not to dominate; it is a complementary foundational gift. According to New Testament ecclesiology, the church is built on this solid foundational structure.

The prophetic word is never to be despised or dismissed, but it is to be harnessed. The "fire" must stay in the fireplace.

Prophets are part of the infrastructure of the church; they are not outside agitators, as some have supposed. Prophets and teachers can work together to build up the body of Christ. All the gifts of the Holy Spirit are necessary, but the power gifts tend to overshadow the more obscure gifts. This becomes problematic for those who wish to build up the body of Christ by exercising their gifts in the assembly. In my estimation prophets need to learn proper protocol, much like people in modern America need to learn proper cell phone etiquette. Most people would be much more receptive to the gift of prophecy if those who function in the realm of the prophetic followed scriptural order. The order encouraged in Paul's letter to the Corinthians is corrective, and it is included because of problems that arose in the early church. New problems have arisen in the present day that must be addressed so the modern church does not despise prophecy because it is neither administered properly nor presented with dignity.

Chapter 19

Discerning *of* Spirits

T HE GIFT OF discerning of spirits is not to be mistaken for a natural intuitive gift of showing good judgment or discernment. The apostle John instructs the church to "test the spirits" to see (discern) whether they are from God (1 John 4:1). Only the spiritually discerning can assess the world of "spirits." So unless one is gifted in this critical area, one is cautioned to leave this work to those who are so gifted and discerning. Those who are looking to mature in this gift should consult the great work of antiquity, *The Spiritual Exercises of St. Ignatius of Loyola*.[1]

When we are talking about discerning spirits, to what kind of spirits are we referring? Let me suggest just a few. Fallen angels are commonly referred to as demon spirits or devils; in some cases they are referred to as unclean spirits. The human spirit has an inclination toward spiritual things; however, it might still be in a comatose state (prior to regeneration), or it might be distorted or perverted. Familiar spirits are conjured up by mediums; the apostle Paul calls these demons. Archangels, seraphim, and cherubim are also recorded in Scripture—there is a whole world of spiritual reality to be discerned. Most important, however, is the person of the Holy Spirit—the third person of the blessed, undivided Trinity, who is on a mission to make the creation of God holy.

Any discussion of discerning of spirits will also lead to the subject of exorcism. Exorcism, which was a rite used early on in the church during baptismal services, acknowledged the need for a cleansing of the whole man. Prayers of renunciation were directed at the devil and his unholy company as a means of freeing the newly "illuminated" individual from the spiritual forces of wickedness. One cannot cast out the flesh—it must be subdued, crucified, and denied. However, spirits must be discerned and in the case of principalities, powers, and rulers of the darkness of this age (Eph. 6:20), expelled. I could relate many stories about discernment and expulsion of demonic powers over cities, churches, and families, but I want to respect the privacy of the individuals involved.

The New International Dictionary of Pentecostal and Charismatic Movements records an important entry by author Peter D. Hocken, PhD, to substantiate the reality of demonic spirits that need to be discerned and expelled. He writes:

> Conscious awareness of the Holy Spirit is typically followed by a new awareness of the reality of Satan and the powers of evil. The spread and development of the movement has led to an increased practice of deliverance and exorcism.[1]

> The spiritual gifts listed in 1 Cor. 12:8–10 were seen from the start as characteristic features of CR [charismatic renewal]. While glossolalia attracted the most attention in the early years, the gifts that have come most to the forefront in the last decade have been prophecy and healing.[2]

Amid all of this charismatic renewal a great deal of discernment must be exercised in order to avoid excesses that, along with some of the scandals of the past,[3] could greatly jeopardize the credibility of the movement. An honest, self-deprecating history is refreshing, and it is the method the Holy Scriptures use to report the events of the past. Discerning what spirits are behind an event can help reveal the fruit the movement will bear. If there is error, being proactive in spiritual warfare will save the day in most cases.

In explaining the gifts of the Spirit for *The New International Dictionary of Pentecostal and Charismatic Movements*, theologian J. Ramsey Michaels, ThD, writes: "The author of 1 John warns his readers not to believe every spirit, but to 'test the spirits to see whether they are from God, because many false prophets have gone out into the world. This is how you know the Spirit of God: Every spirit that confesses that Jesus Christ has come in the flesh is from God, and every spirit that does not confess that Jesus Christ has come in the flesh is not from God. This is the spirit of the antichrist' (1 John 4:1–3; cf. v. 6)."[4]

Many ancient scholars and mystics (too many to list at this time) have warned the faithful in this manner and cautioned them regarding dreams, which were often thought to have spiritual significance. These teachers were not invalidating these experiences, nor were they implying that they belonged only to the apostolic age. They were simply encouraging believers to exercise discernment and not to attribute every spiritual experience to God.

Exploring the spiritual realm can be dangerous, and it is easy to fall into deception. This is why more experienced elders should be consulted when the need arises to delve into this territory. There is a thin line between divine madness and sound spiritual reality. The apostle John wrote of this. The young men he describes in his epistle seemed to be on a power kick whereas the older men in the passage celebrated their relationship with God. Let us examine the Scriptures that reveal this phenomenon:

> I am writing to you, little children, because your sins are forgiven for His name's sake. I am writing to you, fathers,

> because you have known Him who is from the begin-
> ning. I am writing to you, young men, because you have
> overcome the evil one. I am writing to you, little children,
> because you have known the Father. I have written to
> you, fathers, because you have known Him who is from
> the beginning. I have written to you, young men, because
> you are strong, and the word of God lives in you, and you
> have overcome the evil one.
>
> —1 JOHN 2:12–14

Three categorized areas of maturation listed in this text deserve to be commented upon for the sake of clarity. The categories are metaphorical and are marked by neither gender nor age. The first category is that of "dear children"—one can derive from the context that these are new believers who know that their sins are forgiven and that they are restored to the Father. The second category is that of "young men"—a reference that would intimate growth and strength that is being experienced in the spiritual realm. The apostle John tells the young men that they are strong and are overcomers. However, from my vantage point, that is not the end of the matter. The last category is the fathers "who have known Him [God] from the beginning." Believers in this category have a history with God and a level of maturity that allows them to now reproduce and establish other spiritual children. This is the goal—maturation and reproduction born out of an intimate relationship with God.

FACTS ABOUT DISCERNING OF SPIRITS

Discerning of spirits is not having remarkable insight, an aptitude for profound reasoning, or wise judgment.

While these are valuable assets and have their place in our lives, they have nothing to do with the supernatural gift of discerning of spirits. This gift operates only in Spirit-filled believers. The uniting of the Holy Spirit with a believer's human spirit makes it possible for a believer to be aware of spirit entities in his or her vicinity. This awareness is exclusive of any process of mental reasoning. This awareness could cause some to say, "I sensed that something wasn't right." Others might say, "I had a bad vibe."

One could be called "a discerning person." The individual may have discernment in various areas but not have the gift of discerning of spirits. Just as general knowledge differs from the supernatural gift of a word of knowledge, so discernment in general is different from the gift of discerning of spirits. This gift is vital to keep the believer from being deceived; it is our best source of information when engaged in spiritual warfare.

Both good and evil inhabit the unseen world of spirits.

The rulers in this realm are God and the devil. Angels and other heavenly beings do God's will; the evil powers, wicked spirits, and rulers of darkness are under Satan's authority. War between the two is ongoing. One of the weapons God provides His people is the ability to discern between good and evil spirits. He provides this through the supernatural gift of the Spirit called discerning of spirits. The gift distinguishes between four spirits:

1. The Holy Spirit

2. The regenerate human spirit (one who has received Jesus as Savior)

3. The unregenerate human spirit (an unsaved person)

4. Satan and demonic spirits

We are instructed to "test the spirits" (1 John 4:1).

Recognizing whether one is in the presence of a human spirit, an evil spirit, or a heavenly spirit is vital to our spiritual well-being. The early disciples and apostles availed themselves of this gift to make sure they were being led by the Holy Spirit rather than by human or earthly spirits. At the council in Jerusalem the requirements for non-Jewish believers were under dispute. The disciples used spiritual judgment by concluding, "For it seemed good to the Holy Spirit and to us…" (Acts 15:28). Their resolution of the matter was not based on human opinion—of which, I am sure, there were many—but they were able to discern the Holy Spirit's words.

It is prudent to be cautious regarding what manner of spirit one is dealing with since manifestations of the Spirit can be counterfeited.

For example, the sudden transformation of Paul from Jewish persecutor to Christian evangelist would be difficult for most to accept. They would be leery of Paul, thinking he may be trying to trick them. However, because Barnabas had spiritual discernment, all doubts about Paul were settled (Acts 9:26–28). We might wonder why the others did not discern Paul's regenerate spirit—why only Barnabas? The answer lies in 1 Corinthians 12:11, "But that one and very same Spirit works all these, dividing to each one individually as He will."

The gift of discerning of spirits is very important when judging professed inspirational utterances.

The gift enables one to distinguish between the expository preaching of the faithful shepherd of the flock and the sounding brass of the pretender. The gift of discerning of spirits often works with words of wisdom and knowledge to expose and rebuke spirits of error. When James and John wanted to call down fire upon certain people, Jesus rebuked them (Luke 9:54–55). They did not know what spirit they were of. The Bible warns, "Even him, whose coming is in accordance with the working of Satan with all power and signs and false wonders, and with all deception of unrighteousness among those who perish, because they did not receive the love for the truth that they might be saved. Therefore God will send them a strong delusion, that they should believe the lie: That they all might be condemned who did not believe the truth but had pleasure in unrighteousness" (2 Thess. 2:9–12).

The discerning of spirits is God's answer to Satan's deception.

Chapter 20

The Gift *of* Tongues

THE GIFT OF tongues stems from the Day of Pentecost experience. This gift has its roots in the writings of the prophet Isaiah, who foretold that, "With stammering lips and foreign tongue He will speak to this people" (Isa. 28:11). It was to be a sign to the nations.

The gift of tongues is a supernatural manifestation of and miracle from God, though many natural explanations have been offered in modern theological discourse regarding its validity. The apostle Paul sets this gift in the necessary framework when he distinguishes between the corporate expression and the individual, devotional expression of tongues when he says, "I speak in tongues more than you all" (1 Cor. 14:18).

While the gift of tongues has been abused and mishandled, it also has been neglected. Many questions have arisen concerning the "tongues of men and of angels" written of in the Holy Scriptures. Are the tongues we experience coherent "tongues of men and angels" or just gibberish during an esoteric frenzy? Tongues that are characterized as secrets being communicated to God are very mysterious in the sense that they are a "holy mystery." The experience of speaking in tongues is unexplainable, yet it is a valid experience within the Christian context and assembly.

An order and a precedent has been set in the Word of God that creates parameters for the exercise of tongues in a Christian assembly. Two or three people may speak in an unknown tongue, but there must be an interpretation. If no one in the assembly has the gift of interpretation, the speaker in tongues should pray that he can interpret it (1 Cor. 14:13).

"Do all speak in tongues?" This question is raised in 1 Corinthians 12:30 for our consideration, but what is its context? People have tried to use this verse to disprove the validity of speaking in tongues, claiming that 1 Corinthians 12:30 indicates tongues is not for all believers. But the logic they use to make this point is not contextual logic. Again the distinction the apostle Paul makes about devotional tongues and corporate/assembly tongues in 1 Corinthians 14 must be considered in order to understand this passage in 1 Corinthians 12.

Facts About the Gift of Tongues

The gift of tongues is God's idea and operation.

That alone should settle the question for most people who ask why we need the gift of tongues. Jesus said, "These signs will accompany those who believe: In my name they will drive out demons; they will speak in new tongues" (Mark 16:17). The prophet Isaiah said, "Indeed, with stammering lips and foreign tongue He will speak to this people" (Isa. 28:11).

On the Day of Pentecost, the apostles and disciples were gathered in the Upper Room waiting as Jesus had commanded for the "Promise of the Father"—the baptism with the Holy Spirit (Acts 1:4–8). They did not know exactly what they were waiting for, but they waited in obedience to Jesus's command. How surprised they must have been to hear a sound like the rushing of a mighty wind that filled the whole house. Then, likely before they could even ask one another what that sound could be, they saw divided tongues that appeared as fire—and one of these fiery tongues came down and sat upon each person. What a sight that must have been! "And they were all filled with the Holy Spirit and began to speak in other tongues, as the Spirit enabled them to speak" (Acts 2:4). Three key things occurred in that Upper Room:

- They heard the mighty wind.
- They saw the fiery tongues.
- They spoke as the Holy Spirit gave them utterance.

Speaking in tongues can be a sign to unbelievers, as it was on the Day of Pentecost.

The people gathered in Jerusalem on that day were from all over the known world. They heard, each in their own native language, the disciples speaking about the wonderful works of God. They were amazed and perplexed (Acts 2:5–12). The manifestation of speaking in tongues on that day was a sign that salvation in Jesus Christ was available to people of all nations and languages. With this sign God was undoing the confusion and separation that came at the Tower of Babel (Gen. 14:1–9).

One of the outcomes of the charismatic renewal was that people of various cultures and church affiliations found that after receiving the baptism of the Holy Spirit with the sign of speaking in tongues, the old barriers that separated them no longer mattered. The Full Gospel Business Men's Fellowship was highly instrumental in promoting worship and fellowship among believers of various denominations and backgrounds. Spirit-filled believers understood that they were "one in the Spirit" with others, just as Peter understood that the Gentiles who received the Holy Spirit and spoke in tongues at the house of Cornelius were one with the early Christians of Jewish descent (Acts 2:38–39).

The gift of tongues gives believers the ability to speak in languages foreign to them.

Tongues is a supernatural ability, not a learned skill. Those who speak in tongues have deliberately submitted themselves to the Spirit's control. When one speaks in tongues, he or she speaks words that do not originate in the human mind; they come from one's spirit.

One woman shared her experience upon receiving the baptism of the Holy Spirit with the manifestation of speaking in tongues. Analytical by nature, she was extremely curious about what was involved in speaking in tongues. Her first awareness was that the "unknown words and phrases" did not originate in her mind but from "somewhere" in her inner being. The unction to speak flowed upward to her vocal chords, not downward from her mind. To push the analysis still further, she picked up a magazine and began to read even as she continued speaking in tongues. Her mind operated on one level; her inner spirit on another.

When people speak with tongues, the Spirit gives the language while the human speaker submits his or her vocal organs for articulation.

Speaking in tongues edifies and builds up the individual believer when practiced in one's personal prayer devotions.

Paul said that the one who speaks in a tongue speaks to God and edifies himself (1 Cor. 14:2, 4). And Jude says, "Beloved, build yourselves up in your most holy faith. Pray in the Holy Spirit" (v. 20).

So as shown above, this gift of tongues is given by the Lord for the good of the church, the believer, and the world. Together with the gift of interpretation, which we are about to address, the church as a body is edified and instructed. In one's private time in prayer the gift allows the believer to pray from the depths of his or her spirit, enabled by the Holy Spirit, and the world benefits when the gift of tongues is manifested as an earthly language for the communication of the gospel. In all these cases the Lord is glorified and His people edified.

Chapter 21

Interpretation *of* Tongues

THE INTERPRETATION OF tongues presupposes speaking in tongues in a public assembly. There has been much confusion in many circles regarding the dynamics of this gift. The combination of tongues and interpretation in many cases equals the gift of prophecy (1 Cor. 14:5); thus the same guidelines apply: "For you may all prophesy one by one, that all may learn and all may be encouraged" (v. 31). Here again one must distinguish the office of prophet from the member who prophesies. Because *all* can prophesy does not mean that *all* walk in the office of a prophet.

Tongues in the assembly often acts as a trumpet warning, metaphorically announcing the voice of God. The gift of interpretation of tongues is not a word-for-word translation; instead, it is a revelation of the inspiration in the tongue and an expression of the person giving the interpretation. I have observed critics who were counting the number of words in the interpretation, expecting it to act as a word-for-word translation. However, even a translation of a natural language does not always use exactly the same number of words. A person who understands both languages can observe this difference in the interpreter's rendering of a sermon being presented in another language. The person may proclaim many idioms that are more familiar to the culture being addressed.

In the spiritual realm these are mysteries that only God understands, as Scripture declares (v. 2), even if they are the "tongues [or languages] of men and of angels" (1 Cor. 13:1). As discussed previously, the history of this phenomenon is found in the words of the prophet Isaiah: "Indeed, with stammering lips and foreign tongue He will speak to this people" (Isa. 28:11). Although this is a nuance of sorts, the verse does indicate the mysterious way in which God reveals Himself.

A precise explanation is provided by Russell P. Spittler, PhD, in *The New International Dictionary of Pentecostal Charismatic Movements*. It reads as follows:

> The spiritual gift (*charisma*) by which one so endowed makes clear to the congregation the unintelligible utterance of one who has spoken in tongues. This gift, and not speaking in tongues as often stated, appears at the end of three lists of charismata (1 Cor. 12:10, 30; 14:26), not because it is least valued, but because of its necessarily close relation to glossolalia—which it follows immediately in all these places.
>
> Interpretation (*hermeneia*) itself is a charismatic gift, no less extraordinary than any other charisma. The overall corrective pastoral advice given by Paul in 1 Cor. 12-14 calls for the elimination of uninterpreted glossolalia in the congregation (14:5). For this reason, those who speak in tongues should pray for the ability to interpret (v. 13).[1]

He gives further directives with a level of specificity that helps to clarify any confusion about the function of this gift when he says, "But a different person may interpret (v. 27). Since it can be determined if an interpreter is present (v. 28), this charisma may habitually reside with certain persons known for such ability. Not all are interpreters (12:30). Speakers in tongues should not exercise their gift but speak to themselves if no interpreter is present (14:28)."[2]

He then explains the function of the gift as it works together with glossolalia and prophecy: "Interpretation shares with prophecy the end result of an uplifting message that bears meaning for the whole congregation. Coupled with speaking in tongues, the double event gains a sign value when unbelievers are present (v. 22)."[3]

FACTS ABOUT THE GIFT OF INTERPRETATION OF TONGUES

The gift of interpretation of tongues is linked with the gift of tongues.

This gift is a divine enablement and has nothing to do with the learned ability to interpret languages in the natural. Interpretation of tongues is a supernatural gift. The one with this gift does not translate what is spoken in a message in tongues; rather, his or her words are as supernaturally inspired and as dependent on the Holy Spirit for utterance as the gift of tongues. Both are totally dependent on the Spirit of God. While the interpretation will be given in the language of the hearers, the one giving the interpretation will not know ahead of time what the message will be. He, like the hearers, will have the message unfold word by word as he speaks.

The interpretation of tongues need not be a word-for-word translation.

It can be shorter or longer than the message in tongues. When Daniel interpreted the handwriting on the wall to Belshazzar, he used three sentences to explain the meaning of three words (Dan. 5:25–28).

The gift of interpretation of tongues, like the gift of prophecy, is to edify, exhort, correct, and comfort the people of God.

It will not tear down, condemn, or confuse. The gifts of utterance are always to function under the umbrella of love (1 Cor. 13:1–2). To function in this love, spiritual gifts must never offend or impose upon those to whom they minister. This gift is as important for the church of the twenty-first century as it was for the first-century church.

Chapter 22

The Seven Gifts *of* Romans 12

IT IS INTERESTING to note that the gift of prophecy is listed in Romans 12 with a cluster of other gifts that do not seem related to the "power gifts" in other sections of Paul's writings. In the Epistle to the Romans (most likely an earlier epistle than 1 Corinthians), the apostle Paul, the same author who provided the codification in 1 Corinthians 12, seems to provide different categories in listing the gifts in Romans 12:6–8:

> We have diverse gifts according to the grace that is given to us: if prophecy, according to the proportion of (or in agreement with the) faith; if service, in serving; he who teaches, in teaching; he who exhorts, in exhortation; he who gives, with generosity; he who rules, with diligence; he who shows mercy, with cheerfulness.

Note that the passage in Romans 12 lists the following gifts:

+ Prophesying
+ Serving
+ Teaching
+ Encouraging
+ Contributing to the needs of others

+ Leadership
+ Showing mercy

This list of seven tells us a great deal more regarding the work of the person of the Holy Spirit. Traditionally in Pentecostal/ charismatic circles, when one is speaking of spiritual gifts he or she is not referring to this list of seven found in Romans 12, but to the nine gifts of 1 Corinthians 12. The gifts in Romans, although not verbalized as such, would be considered "lesser" gifts by many, with the exception of prophecy, which is considered a superior gift— much sought-after according to 1 Corinthians 14:1, which declares: "Follow after love and desire spiritual gifts, but especially that you may prophesy."

The apostle Paul does not seem to limit the working of the Holy Spirit to a list that one can categorize and see as divisible. This statement does not negate the fact that specific people are endowed with specific gifts; however, in the kingdom of God there are no labor unions where people are restricted to certain areas of functionality. Therefore, when learning about the work of the Holy Spirit, one must be careful not to limit God to a list. The seven gifts mentioned in Romans 12 are important to the edification, care, and nurturing of the church, as are the gifts listed in 1 Corinthians 12.

I would like to take some time to codify and explain their practical function in the life of the church. The gift of prophecy has been explained in other parts of this book; however, there is one comment that must be made in light of the exhortation before us. The thought seems to be that those who prophesy must do so within the confines of their faith (that is, exercising the gift of prophecy according to their personal faith) and not go beyond their ability to believe what they are prophesying. This instruction is explicit; however, in my experience the majority of those who function in this gift have not heeded this warning (regarding exercising the gift of prophecy according to the "proportion" of their personal faith).

The Holy Spirit-inspired gift of *serving* is often downplayed because it is not spectacular in the eyes of man. The gift of *teaching* is sometimes looked upon as a natural talent rather than a spiritual gift. *Encouragement*—something we all need—is sometimes masked in a prophetic word instead of being delivered to the individual who needs it most. *Giving* may work in the same way; one may give to the general fund or may feel the need to give to a specific need or individual.

The gift of *mercy* could bring a balm of healing to many discouraged or hurting members of the body of Christ. *Leadership*, a gift that has been despised and avoided in the past (Isa. 3:7), must be God-inspired and reflect God's eternal and transcendent nature. People will follow with enthusiasm those who reflect and embody godliness and servanthood with competence.

We desperately need a resurgence of these often-neglected gifts in order for the church to be balanced. Yet it is true balance that is the key. For example, it would be wrong for one who shows mercy to say to one who prophesies out of order, "Oh, that's OK. Go ahead." That would not be an expression of the true gift of mercy. These gifts can be very personal, reflecting individual personalities, yet they are for the common good. Their purpose is to glorify almighty God alone.

The apostle Paul was exhibiting the gift of leadership when he helped the church understand the administration and organization (i.e., the order) required for the household of God to function effectively. All that is done in the household of God should be done in the spirit of a servant of God, with humility as unto the Lord, not unto men. That must be undergird all we do.

People do not own the gifts—they are simply stewards of these graces that belong to God alone and are for His glory and honor. Thus the reference we hear so often to "my gifts" is a little misleading. They are God's gifts on loan. They are equipment for the journey. One day they will be taken back after an account for their use has been given to God. Only God is autonomous and all-powerful; humans simply have been given delegated authority and must give an account for their use of it.

What part does character—the workings of the Holy Spirit in cultivating virtue—have in the safekeeping and proper utilization of these gifts? I believe that many people have downplayed and even neglected the "fruit of the Spirit" because they are not associated with the spectacular. This ought not be.

Spiritual gifts are a blessing from God. While the church has always honored their availability, it has not always recognized their Source in reverence and holy fear. I hope that as I presented the material in this book in an academically sound way, I have adequately highlighted the need for reverence and accountability so no one approaches the gifts of the Spirit with disdain and irreverence, as if a formula rather than a stewardship was being discussed. Reverence and the fear of the Lord are an important starting place in any investigation of the mysteries of God!

Chapter 23

Wind, Fire, *and* Water— Important Metaphors *of the* Holy Spirit

DUE TO THE complexities related to understanding the various functions of the person of the Holy Spirit, it is helpful to use metaphors to try to unpack and to explain these great mysteries. I will comment on just a few examples of imagery to set the stage for using metaphor to explain spiritual realities.

A simile is an expression of similarity (i.e., something that is like something is therefore similar to it). So these expressions do not totally represent the function of the person of the Holy Spirit, but they aid in giving insight into His nature. Wind, fire, and water are powerful natural elements that humankind cannot easily control. Many times in Scripture God is likened to something. For example, the Book of Revelation says His eyes were like blazing fire (Rev. 1:14), His voice was like the sound of many waters (v. 15), His feet were like fine brass (v. 15), and so on.

Wind can be refreshing, and it can be destructive. In observing this truth, one can begin to understand the wisdom of God in using tangible realities that humans have experienced to explain eternal realities. Fire brings warmth, but it can also be destructive when not harnessed. Water is even more comprehensive and is an important symbol in the church (i.e., water baptism). Water is cleansing. Like air or wind, water is an absolute necessity. Yet what can we understand about its depths that can crack open some insight for the Christian?

Pictures communicate a thousand words. Jesus, in instructing us about the work of the Holy Spirit, uses the metaphor of wind to explain His activity. The Holy Spirit hovers over the face of the deep, according to the Torah, the Law given by Moses. The Pentateuch (the first five books of the Old Testament) has many references to the activity of the Holy Spirit manifesting in various ways. However, isn't there something impersonal about using raw elements in these metaphors that would depersonalize the person of the Holy Spirit? Let's examine them more closely.

One could not breathe without air. Nor could one survive without water. Fire is a necessary element because of its ability to transform and to burn away the impurities of an object. With water, one can drown if he ingests too much or die of dehydration without it. The Holy Spirit is all of this to the Christian. He is the breath of prayer and the oxygen of love from the heavenly Father.

When a person tries to explain a spiritual experience it can be too difficult for words, and he or she must use metaphor for the sake of brevity; it is just too comprehensive to explain in simple terms. Those who use anthropomorphisms such as the egg or the shamrock to explain the mystery of the Holy Trinity are oversimplifying holy mysteries. The use of metaphors is a more appropriate approach so as not to bring God down to us but to instead elevate our thoughts toward Him. Our God is a consuming fire—how very awesome and fearful is this statement. We must always see that the Holy Spirit is the awesomeness of God. An entire church council was devoted to this important task. The Athanasian Creed highlights this truth:

Whosoever will be saved, before all things it is necessary that he hold the catholic faith. Which faith except everyone do keep whole and undefiled, without doubt he shall perish everlastingly.

And the catholic faith is this, that we worship one God in Trinity and Trinity in Unity. Neither confounding the Persons, nor dividing the Substance. For there is one Person of the Father, another of the Son, and another of the Holy Ghost. But the Godhead of the Father, of the Son, and of the Holy Ghost is all One: the glory equal, the majesty coeternal. Such as the Father is, such is the Son, and such is the Holy Ghost. The Father uncreated, the Son uncreated, and the Holy Ghost uncreated. The Father incomprehensible, the Son incomprehensible, and the Holy Ghost incomprehensible. The Father eternal, the Son eternal, and the Holy Ghost eternal. And yet they are not three Eternals but one Eternal. As there are not Three Uncreated, nor three Incomprehensibles, but one Uncreated and one Uncomprehensible. So likewise the Father is almighty, the Son almighty, and the Holy Ghost almighty. And yet they are not three Almighties, but one Almighty. So the Father is God, the Son is God, and the Holy Ghost is God. And yet they are not three Gods, but one God. So likewise the Father is Lord, the Son Lord, and the Holy Ghost Lord. And yet not three Lords, but one Lord. For like as we are compelled by the Christian verity to acknowledge every Person by Himself to be God and Lord, So are we forbidden by the catholic religion to say, There be three Gods, or three Lords.

The Father is made of none: neither created, nor begotten. The Son is of the Father alone; not made, nor created, but begotten. The Holy Ghost is of the Father and of the Son: neither made, nor created, nor begotten, but proceeding. So there is one Father, not three Fathers; one Son, not Three Sons; one Holy Ghost, not three Holy Ghosts. And in this Trinity none is before or after other; none is greater or less than another; But the whole three Persons are coeternal together, and coequal: so that in all things, as is aforesaid, the Unity in Trinity and the Trinity in Unity is to be worshipped. He, therefore, that will be saved must thus think of the Trinity.

Furthermore, it is necessary to everlasting salvation that he also believe faithfully [or rightly] the incarnation of our Lord Jesus Christ. For the right faith is, that we believe and confess that our Lord Jesus Christ, the Son of God, is God and Man; God of the Substance of the Father, begotten before the worlds; and Man of the substance of His mother, born into the world; Perfect God and perfect Man, of a reasonable soul and human flesh subsisting. Equal to the Father as touching His Godhead, and inferior to the Father as touching His manhood; Who, although He be God and Man, yet He is not two, but one Christ: One, not by conversion of the Godhead into flesh, but by taking of the manhood into God; One altogether; not by confusion of Substance, but by unity of Person. For as the reasonable soul and flesh is one man, so God and Man is one Christ; Who suffered for our salvation; descended into hell, rose again the third day from the dead; He ascended into heaven; He sitteth on the right hand of the Father, God Almighty; from whence He shall come to judge the quick and the dead. At whose coming all men shall rise again with their bodies, and shall give an account of their own works. And they that

> have done good shall go into life everlasting; and they
> that have done evil, into everlasting fire.
>
> This is the catholic faith; which except a man believe
> faithfully and firmly, he cannot be saved.[1]

In my estimation this creed, attributed to St. Athanasius (293–373), the great hero of the Council of Nicea,[2] is the clearest theological statement regarding the person of the Holy Spirit and His relationship to the undivided, blessed Holy Trinity.

In the preceding pages it has been my desire to clarify some misunderstandings concerning the Person, work, gift, and gifts of the Holy Spirit. It is my hope that I have accomplished this in some small way. I have emphasized the difference between the Giver of the gifts, the Holy Spirit, and the gifts themselves. As stated above it seems to be in the nature of man that he is many times more enamored with the supernatural works and gifts of the Spirit than he is with the Holy Spirit Himself, which tends to lead to misuse and abuse. Again I want to state that the Holy Spirit is not an "it" but rather a divine Person—a divine Person within the communion of the one Godhead, the Holy Trinity. Augustine was known to teach that the members of the Holy Trinity were held together in communion by love and that that divine love was the Holy Spirit. Therefore, every work that flows from the Godhead flows from that divine love.

The gifts of the Holy Spirit are gifts of love from a loving Father in a loving Son through the loving Spirit. It is no coincidence that 1 Corinthians 13, the great chapter of love, serves as a bridge between the apostle Paul's teaching listing some of the gifts in 1 Corinthians 12 and his teaching regulating the use of those gifts in the church in 1 Corinthians 14. Therefore, whenever we choose to submit ourselves to the Lord and become loving and holy vessels fit for the manifestation of His spiritual gifts, we must always choose to exercise them in His divine love. If we do this, then the Lord—the Father, Son, and Holy Spirit—will receive the glory and honor due to Him, His people will be edified, and a love-starved world will behold His hand of love working among them.

Notes

CHAPTER 2

1. Stanley M. Burgess and Eduard M. van der Maas, eds., *The New International Dictionary of Pentecostal and Charismatic Movements* (Grand Rapids, MI: Zondervan, 2002), 667.

CHAPTER 3

1. Joseph T. McGloin, *A Manual of Prayers—Pontifical North American College* (Huntington, IN: Our Sunday Visitor, 1998).
2. Ibid.
3. Ibid.; St. Bonaventure, "Prayer of St. Bonaventure to the Holy Spirit," http://www.sanbuenaventuramission.org/history/st-bonaventure (accessed April 28, 2014).
4. McGloin, *A Manual of Prayers—Pontifical North American College.*
5. Ibid.; Otto Zardetti, *Special Devotion to the Holy Ghost: A Manual for the Use of Seminarians* (Milwaukee, WI: Hoffman Brothers, 1888), 157.
6. Catholic Online, "Come Holy Spirit," http://www.catholic.org/prayers/prayer.php?p=331 (accessed April 28, 2014).
7. Ibid.
8. St. James Vicariate for Hebrew Speaking Catholics in Israel, "Veni Creator Spiritus—a Prayer to the Holy Spirit," May 25, 2012, http://www.catholic.co.il/index.php?option=com_content&view=article&id=401%3Aveni-creator-spiritus-a-prayer-to-the-holy-spirit&catid=31%3Aprayers&Itemid=43&lang=en (accessed April 28, 2014); Veli-Matti Kärkkäinen, *The Holy Spirit: A Guide to Christian Theology* (Louisville, KY: Westminster John Knox Press, 2012), 35.

CHAPTER 5

1. St. Ambrose of Milan, "On the Holy Spirit," The Crossroads Initiative, https://www.crossroadsinitiative.com/library_article/658/On_the_Holy_Spirit__Book_I_St_Ambrose_of_Milan.html (accessed

April 30, 2014); Encyclopedia Britannica, "Saint Ambrose," http://www.britannica.com/EBchecked/topic/19014/Saint-Ambrose (accessed April 30, 2014).

2. Hermas, *The Shepherd of Hermas*, NewAdvent.org, http://www.newadvent.org/fathers/02012.htm (accessed April 30, 2014).

3. Ibid.

4. Irenaeus, *Against Heresies*, NewAdvent.org, http://www.newadvent.org/fathers/0103509.htm (accessed April 30, 2014).

5. Ibid.

6. Encyclopedia Britannica, "Tertullian," http://www.britannica.com/EBchecked/topic/588511/Tertullian (accessed April 30, 2014).

7. Encyclopedia Britannica, "Origen," http://www.britannica.com/EBchecked/topic/432455/Origen (accessed April 30, 2014).

8. Encyclopedia Britannica, "Saint Clement of Alexandria," http://www.britannica.com/EBchecked/topic/121112/Saint-Clement-of-Alexandria (accessed April 30, 2014).

9. Origen, *De Principiis*, NewAdvent.org, http://www.newadvent.org/fathers/04122.htm (accessed April 30, 2014).

CHAPTER 6

1. Peter Lombard, *The Four Books of Sentences* (N.p: n.d).

CHAPTER 8

1. Nicene Creed, Spurgeon.org, http://www.spurgeon.org/~phil/creeds/nicene.htm (accessed April 30, 2014).

2. Every effort was made to identify the source of this prayer, but its origin is unknown.

3. Ibid.

4. Ibid.

5. Ibid.

CHAPTER 9

1. Nicene Creed, *The Book of Common Prayer* (N.p.: Don C. Warrington, 2004), 145–146, http://www.vulcanhammer.org/anglican/bcp-1662.pdf (accessed April 30, 2014).

2. JoHannah Reardon, "The Nicene and Apostles' Creeds," Chris tianityToday.com, July 30, 2008, http://www.christianitytoday .com/biblestudies/articles/churchhomeleadership/080730.html (accessed April 30, 2014).

3. S. Michael Houdmann, "What Is the Filioque Clause/Filioque Controversy," GotQuestions.org, http://www.gotquestions.org/ filioque-clause-controversy.html (accessed April 30, 2014).

4. Scott P. Richert, "Reader Question: Why Holy Ghost?" About.com, May 28, 2009, http://catholicism.about.com/b/2009/05/28/reader -question-why-holy-ghost.htm (accessed April 30, 2014).

CHAPTER 10

1. Robert A. Evans and Thomas D. Parker, editors, *Christian Theology: A Case Method Approach* (Eugene, OR: Wipf & Stock Publishers, 2001), 159.

2. Ibid.

CHAPTER 12

1. Greek Archdiocese of America, "Speaking in Tongues: An Orthodox Perspective," http://www.goarch.org/ourfaith/our faith7112 (accessed May 1, 2014). In "Speaking in Tongues: An Orthodox Perspective" Father George Nicozisin writes: "Speaking in tongues, *glossolalia*, a popular practice with many churches today, is a phenomenon which can be traced to the days of the Apostles. A decade ago speaking in tongues was encountered only in Pentecostal churches, revival meetings, Quaker gatherings and some Methodist groups. Today *glossolalia* is also found in some Roman Catholic and Protestant churches."

2. Verna Linzey, *Spirit Baptism*, "Tool 41—8 Purposes of Speaking in Tongues," (Maitland, FL: Xulon Press, 2008), 90.

CHAPTER 15

1. Though the gift of faith is listed in both 1 Corinthians 12:4–11 and Romans 12:4–8, it is important to point out that traditionally the seven gifts listed in Isaiah 11:1–2 are different from the gifts of the Holy Spirit promulgated by "classical" Pentecostal Christians.

The Catechism of the Council of Trent says the following in this regard: "The Prophet (Isaias), however, enumerates the chief effects which are most properly ascribed to the Holy Ghost: The spirit of wisdom and understanding, the spirit of counsel and fortitude, the spirit of knowledge and piety, and the spirit of the fear of the Lord. These effects are called the gifts of the Holy Ghost, and sometimes they are even called the Holy Ghost. Wisely, therefore, does St. Augustine admonish us, whenever we meet the word Holy Ghost in Scripture, to distinguish whether it means the Third Person of the Trinity or His gifts and operations. The two are as far apart as the Creator is from the creature." For the full text of The Catechism at the Council of Trent, see http://www.clerus.org/bibliaclerusonline/en/c1h.htm (accessed May 1, 2014).

CHAPTER 18

1. It is not unreasonable to speculate that the four women who prophesied would have voiced their sentiments along with the rest, since it can be assumed from their ministry that they were used to conveying the mind of the Lord and their burdens in public.

2. A noteworthy caution when commenting on these verses (1 Thess. 5:19–21) is found in the 2011 Revised New American Bible, which reads: "Paul's buoyant encouragement of charismatic freedom sometimes occasioned excesses that he or others had to remedy" (see 1 Cor. 14; 2 Thess. 2:1–15; 2 Pet. 3:1–16). This does not invalidate the imperative to "not quench the Spirit" (1 Thess. 5:19, RNAB).

3. See also The Pioneers New Testament, "Word Study #44—Preachers, Priests," http://pioneernt.wordpress.com/2010/04/19/word-study-44-preachers-priests/ (accessed May 2, 2014).

CHAPTER 19

1. Burgess and van der Maas, eds., *The New International Dictionary of Pentecostal and Charismatic Movements*, 515.

2. Ibid., "Charismatic Movement: 7. Spiritual Gifts," 515.

3. A cursory reading of Pentecostal history will provide the reader with much to contemplate regarding credibility and integrity. However, just because there is a fly in the ointment does not mean that we throw out all of the good that is left over. (See: Ecclesiastes

10:1.) Someone has related the truth that the church is like Noah's Ark—it stinks a little, but it is the real thing!

4. Burgess and van der Maas, eds., *The New International Dictionary of Pentecostal and Charismatic Movements*, 665.

CHAPTER 21

1. Burgess and van der Maas, eds., *The New International Dictionary of Pentecostal and Charismatic Movements*, 801.

2. Ibid.

3. Ibid.

CHAPTER 23

1. The Athanasian Creed, *The Book of Concord*, http://bookofconcord .org/creeds.php (accessed May 5, 2014).

2. Encyclopedia Britannica, "Saint Athanasius," http://www.britan nica.com/EBchecked/topic/40590/Saint-Athanasius (accessed May 5, 2014).

Bibliography

Primary Material

Mark the Monk. *Counsels on the Spiritual Life. Vol. 1.* Translated by Tim Vivian. *Vol. 2.* Translated by Tim Vivian and Augustine Casiday. Crestwood, NY: St. Vladimir's Seminary Press, 2009.

St. Basil of Caesarea. *On the Holy Spirit.* Translated by David Anderson. Crestwood, NY: St. Vladimir's Seminary Press, 1980.

St. Irenaeus of Lyons. *Against Heresies.* Translated ANF 1, 1885. Grand Rapids, MI: Eerdmans, 1987.

St. Macarius of Egypt. *Intoxicated With God: The Fifty Spiritual Homilies of Macarius.* Translated by George A. Maloney. Denville, NJ: Dimension Books, 1978.

St. Nicodemos of the Holy Mountain. *Concerning Frequent Communion of the Immaculate Mysteries of Christ.* Translated by. George Dokos. Dalles, OR: Uncut Mountain Press, 2006.

———. *Exomologetarion: A Manual of Confession.* Translated by George Dokos. Dalles, OR: Uncut Mountain Press, 2006.

———. *The Philokalia.* Translated by G. E. H. Palmer, Philip Sherard, Kalistos Ware. London: Faber and Faber Limited, 1977–1995.

St. Photios of Constantinople. *On the Mystagogy of the Holy Spirit.* Translated by the Holy Transfiguration Monastery. Astoria, NY: Studion Publishers, 1983.

St. Symeon the New Theologian. *The Discourses.* Translated by . C. J. deCatanzaro. New York: Paulist Press, 1980.

———. *The First Created Man.* Translated by Seraphim Rose. Platina, CA: St. Herman of Alaska Brotherhood, 1994.

———. *Hymns of Divine Love.* Translated by George Maloney. Denville, NJ: Dimension Books, 1976.

———. *Letter on Confession.* Translated by George Gabriel. Dewdney,

BC: Synaxis Press, 1997.

———. *On the Mystical Life: The Ethical Discourses.* Translated by Alexander Golitzin. 3 vols. Crestwood, NY: St. Vladimir's Seminary Press, 1995–1997.

———. *The Practical and Theological Chapters and the Three Theological Discourses.* Translated by Paul McGuckin. Kalamazoo, MI: Cistercian Publications, 1982.

Secondary Sources

Abbott, Walter M. *The Documents of Vatican II.* London: Geoffrey Chapman, 1966.

Afanasiev, Nicholas. *The Church of the Holy Spirit.* Notre Dame, IN: University of Notre Dame Press, 2007.

Alert, Craig D. *A High View of Scripture?* Grand Rapids, MI: Baker Academic, 2007.

Alexander, Donald L. *Christian Spirituality: Five Views of Sanctification.* Downers Grove: IL: InterVarsity Press, 1988.

Alfeyev, Hilarion. *St. Symeon the New Theologian and Orthodox Tradition.* Oxford: Oxford University Press, 2000.

Altschul, Paisius, ed. *An Unbroken Circle: Linking Ancient African Christianity to the African-American Experience.* St. Louis: Brotherhood of St. Moses the Black, 1997.

———. *Wade in the River: The Story of the African Christian Faith.* Kansas City, MO: Cross Bearers, 2001.

Anagnostopoulos, Stephanos K. *Experiences During the Divine Liturgy.* Piraeus, Greece: G. Gelbesis Publications, 2008.

Anderson, Allan H. *African Reformation: African Initiated Christianity in the 20th Century.* Trenton, NJ: Africa World Press, 2001.

———. *An Introduction to Pentecostalism: Global Charismatic Christianity.* Cambridge: Cambridge University Press, 2004.

———. *Spreading Fires: The Missionary Nature of Early Pentecostalism.* Maryknoll, NY: Orbis Books, 2007.

Archer, Kenneth J. *A Pentecostal Hermeneutic of the Twenty-First Century: Spirit, Scripture and Community.* London: T & T Clark, 2004.

Anderson, Robert Mapes. *Vision of the Disinherited.* New York: Oxford University Press, 1979.

Azkoul, Michael. *Once Delivered to the Saints: An Orthodox Apology for the New Millennium.* Seattle, WA: Saint Nectarios Press, 2000.

Badcock, Gary. *Light of Truth & Fire of Love: A Theology of the Holy Spirit.* Grand Rapids, MI: Eerdmans, 1997.

Bagiackas, Joseph. *The Future Glory: The Charismatic Renewal and the Implementation of Vatican II.* South Bend, IN: Charismatic Renewal Services, 1983.

Bajis, Jordan. *Common Ground: An Introduction to Eastern Christianity for the American Christian.* Minneapolis, MN: Light & Life Publishing, 1996.

Barnett, Donald Lee, and Jeffrey P. McGregor. *Speaking in Tongues: A Scholarly Defense.* Seattle: Community Chapel Publications, 1986.

Barnett, Maurice. *The Living Flame: Being a Study of the Gift of the Spirit in the New Testament.* London: Epsworth Press, 1953.

Bartholomew, Patriarch of Constantinople. *Encountering the Mystery: Understanding Orthodox Christianity Today.* New York: Doubleday, 2008.

Bartleman, Frank. *How Pentecost Came to Los Angeles.* Los Angeles: F. Bartleman, 1925.

Barton. Stephen C., ed. *Holiness: Past and Present.* London: T & T Clark, 2003.

Basham, Don. *Face Up with a Miracle.* Monroeville, PA: Whitaker House, 1971.

———. *A Handbook on Holy Spirit Baptism.* New Kensington, PA: Whitaker House, 1999.

———. *The Miracle of Tongues.* Old Tappan, NJ: Fleming H. Revell, 1973.

Bassett, Paul M. and William M. Greathouse. *The Historical Develop-*

ment. Vol. 1 of *Exploring Christian Holiness.* Kansas City, MO: Beacon Hill Press, 1985.

Bauman, Michael and Martin I. Klauber, eds., *Historians of the Christian Tradition.* Nashville: Broadman & Holman Publishers, 1995.

Beacham, Doug. *G. B. Cashwell.* Franklin Springs, GA: LifeSprings Resources, 2006.

Bennett, Dennis and Rita. *The Holy Spirit and You.* Plainfield, NJ: Logos International, 1971.

———. *How to Pray for the Release of the Holy Spirit.* Plainfield, NJ: Logos International, 1985.

———. *Nine O'clock in the Morning.* Plainfield, NJ: Logos International, 1970.

Bernard, David K. *Practical Holiness: A Second Look.* Vol. IV of Series in Pentecostal Theology. Hazelwood, MO: World Aflame Press, 1985.

Bilaniuk, Petro B. T. *Theology and Economy of the Holy Spirit: An Eastern Approach.* Bangalore, India: Dharmaram Publications, 1980.

Bishops' Liaison Committee With the Catholic Charismatic Renewal. *A Pastoral Statement on the Catholic Charismatic Renewal.* Washington DC: Office of Publishing and Promotion Services, United States Catholic Conference, 1984.

Bittlinger, Arnold, ed. *The Church is Charismatic: The World Council of Churches and the Charismatic Renewal.* Geneva: WCC Renewal and Congregational Life, 1981.

Bixler, R. H., ed. *The Spirit Is-a-Movin'.* Carol Stream, IL: Creation House, 1974.

Blane, Andrew, ed. *Georges Florovsky: Russian Intellectual, Orthodox Churchman.* Crestwood, NY: St. Vladimir's Seminary Press, 1993.

Blumhofer, Edith L., Russell P. Spittler, and Grant Wacker, eds. *Pentecostal Currents in American Protestantism.* Urbana, IL: University of Illinois Press, 1999.

Boone, Pat. *A New Song.* Carol Stream, IL: Creation House, 1970.

Borlase, Craig. *William Seymour: A Biography.* Lake Mary, FL: Charisma House, 2006.

Bradford, Brick. *Releasing the Power of the Holy Spirit.* Oklahoma City, OK: Presbyterian Charismatic Communion, 1983.

Brand, Chad Owen. *Perspectives on Spirit Baptism.* Nashville: Broadman & Holman, 2004.

Brandt, Robert L. and Zenas J. Bicket. *The Spirit Helps Us Pray: A Biblical Theology of Prayer.* Springfield, MO: Gospel Publishing House, 1993.

Braun, John. *Divine Energy: The Orthodox Path to Christian Victory.* Ben Lomond, CA: Conciliar Press, 1991.

Breck, John. *Scripture in Tradition: The Bible and Its Interpretation on the Orthodox Church.* Crestwood, NY: St. Vladimir's Seminary Press, 2001.

Bredesen, Harald. *Yes, Lord.* Plainfield, NJ: Logos International, 1972.

Brooks, Noel. *Scriptural Holiness.* Franklin Springs, GA: Advocate Press, 1967.

Brown, Dale. *Understanding Pietism.* Nappanee, IN: Evangel Publishing House, 1996.

Bruce, F. F. *Tradition: Old and New.* Grand Rapids, MI: Zondervan, 1970.

Brunk II, George R. ed. *Encounter With the Holy Spirit.* Scottsdale, PA: Herald Press, 1972.

Budgen, Victor. *The Charismatics and the Word of God.* Hertfordshire, England: Evangelical Press, 1985.

Bulgakov, Sergius. *The Comforter.* Grand Rapids, MI: Eerdmans, 2004.

———. *The Orthodox Church.* Crestwood, NY: St. Vladimir's Press, 1988.

Bullock, Warren D. and George O. Wood. *When the Spirit Speaks: Making Sense of Tongues, Interpretation & Prophecy.* Springfield, MO: Gospel Publishing House, 2009.

Burdon, Adrian. *Authority and Order: John Wesley and His Preachers.* Hants, England: Ashgate Publishing, 2005.

Burgess, Stanley, ed. *Encyclopedia of Pentecostal and Charismatic Christianity.* New York: Routledge, 2006.

———. *The Holy Spirit: Ancient Christian Traditions.* Peabody, MA: Hendrickson Publishers, 1984.

———. *The Holy Spirit: Eastern Christian Traditions.* Peabody, MA: Hendrickson Publishers, 1989.

———. *The Holy Spirit: Medieval Roman Catholic and Reformation Traditions.* Peabody, MA: Hendrickson Publishers, 1997.

———. ed. *The New International Dictionary of Pentecostal Charismatic Movements.* Grand Rapids, MI: Zondervan, 2002.

Butler, C. S. *Test the Spirits: An Examination of the Charismatic Phenomenon.* Hertfordshire, England: Evangelical Press, 1985.

Byrne, James E. *Living in the Spirit: A Handbook on Catholic Charismatic Christianity.* New York: Paulist Press, 1975.

Cabie, Robert. *The Eucharist.* Vol. 2 of *The Church at Prayer.* Edited by A. G Martimort. Translated by Matthew J. O'Connell. Collegeville, MN: Liturgical Press, 1986.

Campbell, Bob. *Baptism in the Holy Spirit: Command or Option?* Monroeville, PA: Whitaker Books, 1973.

Campbell, Joseph E. *What to Believe and Why About Sanctification.* Franklin Springs, GA: The Publishing House, 1952.

Cantalamessa, Raniero. *Come, Creator Spirit: Meditations on Veni Creator.* Collegeville, MN: Liturgical Press, 2003.

Carteledge, Mark J. *Encountering the Spirit: The Charismatic Tradition.* Maryknoll, NY: Orbis Book, 2006.

Carter, Howard. *Gifts of the Holy Spirit.* Springfield, MO: Gospel Publishing House, 1946.

———. *Spiritual Gifts and Their Operation.* Springfield, MO: Gospel Publishing House, 1991.

Chan, Simon. *Pentecostal Theology and the Christian Spiritual Tradition.* Sheffield, England: Sheffield Academic Press, 2000.

Chervin, Ronda. *Why I Am a Charismatic: A Catholic Explains.*

Liguori, MO: Liguori Publications, 1978.

Cho, Paul Yongi with Harold Hostetler. *Successful Home Cell Groups.* South Plainfield, NJ: Bridge Publishing, 1981.

Chondropoulos, Sotos. *Saint Nekarios-The Saint of Our Century.* Translated by Peter and Aliki Los. Athens, Greece: Kainouragia Ge Publications, 1977.

Christensen, Damascene. *Father Seraphim Rose: His Life and Works.* Platina, CA: St. Herman of Alaska Brotherhood, 2003.

Christensen, Michael J., and Jeffrey A. Wittung, eds. *Partakers of the Divine Nature: The History and Development of Deification in the Christian Traditions.* Grand Rapids, MI: Baker Books, 2007.

Christenson, Larry. *The Charismatic Renewal Among Lutherans.* Minneapolis, MN: Lutheran Charismatic Renewal Services, 1975.

———. *A Message to the Charismatic Renewal.* Weymouth, MA: Dimension, 1972.

———. *Welcome, Holy Spirit: A Study of Charismatic Renewal in the Church.* Minneapolis, MN: Augsburg Publishing House, 1987.

Cirlot, Felix L. *The Early Eucharist.* London: SPCK, 1939.

Clark, Steve. *Baptized in the Spirit and Spiritual Gifts.* Pecos, NM: Dove Publications & Ann Arbor, MI: Servant Books, 1976.

Collins, Kenneth J. *The Scripture Way of Salvation: The Heart of John Wesley's Theology.* Nashville: Abingdon Press, 1997.

Committee for Pastoral Research and Practice, National Conference of Catholic Bishops. *Statement on Catholic Charismatic Renewal.* Washington, DC: Publications Office, United States Catholic Conference, 1975.

Congar, Yves. *I Believe in the Holy Spirit.* Translated by David Smith. 3 vols. New York: Seabury Press, 1983.

———. *The Meaning of Tradition.* Translated by A. N. Woodrow. New York: Hawthorn Books, 1964.

———. *Report From Rome II: The Second Session of the Vatican Council.* London: Geoffrey Chapman, 1964.

————. *Tradition and Traditions: A Historical and Theological Essay.* Translated by Michael Naseby & Thomas Rainborough. New York: The Macmillan Co., 1967.

Coniaris, Anthony. *Achieving Your Potential in Christ: Theosis.* Minneapolis, MN: Light & Life Publishing, 1993.

————. *Introducing the Orthodox Church: Its Faith and Life.* Minneapolis, MN: Light & Life Publishing, 1982.

Cooke, Bernard. *Power and the Spirit of God: Toward an Experience-Based Pneumatology.* Oxford: Oxford University Press, 2004.

Cordes, Paul Josef. *Call to Holiness: Reflections on the Catholic Charismatic Renewal.* Collegeville, MN: Liturgical Press, 1997.

Corey, George S., Peter E. Gilquist, Anne Glynn Mackoul, Jean Sam, Paul Schneirla, eds. *The First One Hundred Years: A Centennial Anthology Celebrating Antiochian Orthodoxy in North America.* Englewood, NJ: Antakya Press, 1995.

Cox, Harvey. *Fire From Heaven : The Rise of Pentecostal Spirituality and the Reshaping of Religion in the 21st Century.* Cambridge, MA: De Capo Press, 2001.

Crowe, Terrence Robert. *Pentecostal Unity: Recurring Frustration and Enduring Hopes.* Chicago: Loyola University Press, 1993.

Davies, J. G. *The Spirit, the Church and the Sacraments.* London: The Faith Press, 1954.

Dayton, Donald W. *Theological Roots of Pentecostalism.* Peabody, MA: Hendrickson Publishers, 1987.

————. and Robert K. Johnston. *The Variety of American Evangelicalism.* Knoxville, TN: University of Tennessee Press, 1991.

Dempster, Murray W., Byron D. Klaus, and Douglas Petersen, eds. *The Globalization of Pentecostalism: A Religion Made to Travel.* Oxford: Regnum Books, 1999.

Derstine, Gerald. *Following the Fire.* Plainfield, NJ: Logos International, 1980.

————. *Visitation of God to the Mennonites.* Bradenton, FL: Gospel

Crusade, 1961.

Dieter, Melvin. *The Holiness Revival of the Nineteenth Century.* Lanham, MD: Scarecrow Press, 1996.

Dillenschneider, Clement. *The Holy Spirit and the Priest: Toward and Interiorization of Our Priesthood.* St. Louis: B. Herder Book Co., 1965.

Dorr, Donal. *Remove the Heart of Stone: Charismatic Renewal and the Experience of Grace.* New York: Paulist Press, 1978.

Du Plessis, David. *A Man Called Mr. Pentecost: David Du Plessis as Told to Bob Slosser.* Plainfield, NJ: Logos International, 1977

———. *The Spirit Bade Me Go.* Plainfield, NJ: Logos International, 1977.

Durasoff, David. *Bright Wind of the Spirit.* New York: Prentice Hall, 1972.

Durham, William. Articles written by Pastor Durham taken from the *Pentecostal Testimony.* Los Angeles: N.p., n.d.

Edwards, Jonathan. *Religious Affections.* Goodyear, AZ: Diggory Press, 2007.

Elbert, Paul, ed. *Essays on Apostolic Themes.* Peabody, MA: Hendrickson Publishers, 1985.

El-Meskeen, Matta. *Orthodox Prayer Life: The Interior Way.* Crestwood, NY: St. Vladimir's Seminary Press, 2003.

Elowsky, Joel C., ed. *We Believe in the Holy Spirit. Vol. 4 of Ancient Christian Doctrine.* Downers Grove, IL; InterVarsity Press, 2009.

Ensley, Eddie. *Sounds of Wonder: A Popular History of Speaking in Tongues in the Catholic Tradition.* New York: Paulist Press, 1977.

Erb, Peter C., ed. *Pietists—Selected Writings.* New York: Paulist Press, 1983.

Ervin, Howard M. *These Are Not Drunken As Ye Suppose.* Plainfield, NJ: Logos, 1967.

Faupel, D. William. *The Everlasting Gospel.* Sheffield, England: Sheffield Academic Press, 1996.

Fee, Gordon D. *Listening to the Spirit in the Text.* Grand Rapids, MI:

Eerdmans, 2000.

Ferguson, Charles W. *Methodists and the Making of America: Organizing to Beat the Devil.* Austin, TX: Eakin Press, 1983.

Fields, Anne. *From Darkness to Light: How One Became a Christian in the Early Church.* Ben Lomond, CA: Conciliar Press, 1997.

Flannery, Austin, ed. *Vatican Council II: The Conciliar and Post Conciliar Documents.* Grand Rapids, MI: Eerdmans, 1992.

———. *Vatican Council II: More Post Conciliar Documents.* Collegeville, MN: The Liturgical Press, 1982.

Florovsky, Georges. *Aspects of Church History.* Belmont, MA: Nordland Publishing, 1975.

———. *Bible, Church, Tradition: An Eastern Orthodox View.* Vaduz, Europa: Buchervertriebsanstalt, 1987.

———. *The Byzantine Ascetic and Spiritual Fathers.* Vaduz, Europa: Buchervertriebsanstalt, 1987.

———. *The Byzantine Fathers of the Fifth Century.* Vaduz, Europa: Buchervertriebsanstalt, 1987.

———. *The Byzantine* Fathers *of the Sixth to the Eighth Century.* Vaduz, Europa: Buchervertriebsanstalt, 1987.

———. *Christianity and Culture.* Belmont, MA: Nordland Publishing, 1974.

———. *Creation and Redemption.* Belmont, MA: Nordland Publishing, 1976.

———. *The Eastern Fathers of the Fourth Century.* Vaduz, Europa: Buchervertriebsanstalt, 1987.

———. *Ecumenism I: A Doctrinal Approach.* Vaduz, Europa: Buchervertriebsanstalt, 1987.

———. *Ecumenism II: A Historical Approach.* Vaduz, Europa: Buchervertriebsanstalt, 1987.

———. *The Ways of Orthodox Theology: Part One.* Belmont: MA: Nordland Publishing, 1979.

———. *The Ways of Orthodox Theology: Part Two.* Vaduz, Europa:

Buchervertriebsanstalt, 1987.

Ford, J. Massingberd. *The Spirit and the Human Person: A Meditation.* Dayton, OH: Pflaum Press, 1969.

Foster, K. Neill. *Help! I Believe in Tongues: A Third View of the Charismatic Phenomenon.* Minneapolis, MN: Bethany Fellowship, 1975.

Frodsham, Stanley. *With Signs Following: The Story of the Pentecostal Revival in the Twentieth Century.* Springfield, MO: Gospel Publishing House, 1946.

Frost, Evelyn. *Christian Healing.* London: A. R. Mowbray, 1940.

Frost, Robert. *Aglow With the Spirit.* Plainfield, NJ: Logos International, 1971.

―――. *Overflowing Life.* Plainfield, NJ: Logos International, 1972.

―――. *Set My Spirit Free.* Plainfield, NJ: Logos International, 1973.

Fudge, Thomas A. *Christianity Without the Cross: A History of Salvation in Oneness Pentecostalism.* Parkland, FL: Universal Publishing, 2003.

Gee, Donald. *Concerning Spiritual Gifts.* Springfield, MO: Gospel Publishing House, 1972.

Gelpi, Donald. *Charism and Sacrament: A Theology of Christian Conversion.* New York: Paulist Press, 1976.

―――. *Pentecostalism: A Theological Viewpoint.* New York: Paulist Press, 1971.

Gilbertson, Richard. *The Baptism of the Holy Spirit: The Views of A.B. Simpson and His Contemporaries.* Camp Hill, PA: Christian Publications, 1993.

Gilet, Lev. *Orthodox Spirituality: An Outline of the Orthodox Ascetical and Mystical Tradition.* Crestwood, NY: St. Vladimir's Seminary Press, 1987.

―――. *The Year of Grace of the Lord.* Crestwood, NY: St. Vladimir's Seminary Press, 1980.

Goergen, Donald J. *Fire of Love: Encountering the Holy Spirit.* New York: Paulist Press, 2006.

Goff, James R. and Wacker, Grant, eds., *Portrait of a Generation: Early Pentecostal Leaders.* Fayetteville, AR: University of Arkansas Press, 2002.

———. *White Unto Harvest: Charles F. Parham and the Missionary Origins of Pentecostalism.* Fayetteville, AR: University of Arkansas Press, 1988.

Goss, Ethel E. *The Winds of God.* Hazelwood, MO: World Aflame Press, 1958.

Gresham Jr., John L. *Charles G. Finney's Doctrine of the Baptism of the Holy Spirit.* Peabody, MA: Hendrickson, 1987.

Grudem, Wayne. *The Gift of Prophecy in the New Testament and Today.* Wheaton, IL: Crossway, 1988.

Gundry, Stanley and James Stamoolis, eds. *Three Views on Eastern Orthodoxy and Evangelicalism.* Grand Rapids, MI: Zondervan, 2004.

Hamilton, Michael P., ed. *The Charismatic Movement.* Grand Rapids, MI: Eerdmans, 1975.

Hanson, R. P. C. *Tradition in the Early Church.* London: SCM Press LTD, 1962.

Harakas, Stanley Samuel. *Of Life and Salvation: Reflections on Living the Christian Life.* Minneapolis, MN: Light & Life, 1996.

Harper, Michael. *As at the Beginning: The Twentieth-Century Pentecostal Revival.* London: Hodder and Stoughton, 1965.

———. *A Faith Fulfilled: Why Are Christians Across Great Britain Embracing Orthodoxy?* Ben Lomond, CA: Conciliar Press, 1999.

———. *Power for the Body of Christ.* England: Fountain Trust, 1965.

Harrell Jr., David Edwin. *All Things Are Possible: The Healing and Charismatic Revivals in Modern America.* Bloomington, IN: Indiana University Press, 1975.

Harris, Ralph. *Acts Today: Signs and Wonders of the Holy Spirit.* Springfield, MO: Gospel Publishing House, 1998.

———. *Spoken by the Spirit: Documented Accounts of "Other Tongues" From Arabic to Zulu.* Springfield, MO: Gospel Publishing House,

1973.

Hath, Alden. *A Man Called John: The Life of Pope John XXIII*. New York: Hawthorn Books, 1963.

Haughey, John C. *The Conspiracy of God the Holy Spirit in Men*. Garden City, NY: Doubleday, 1973.

———. ed. *Theological Reflections on the Charismatic Renewal*. Ann Arbor, MI: Servant Books, 1978.

Hausherr, Irénée. *The Name of Jesus*. Kalamazoo, MI: Cistercian Publications, 1978.

———. *Spiritual Direction in the Early Christian East*. Kalamazoo, MI: Cistercian Publications, 1990.

Hayford, Jack W. *The Beauty of Spiritual Language*. Dallas: Word Publishing, 1992.

———. and S. David Moore. *The Charismatic Century: The Enduring Impact of the Azusa Street Revival*. New York: Time Warner, 2006.

Hazim, Patriarch Ignatius IV. *The Resurrection and Modern Man*. Crestwood, NY: St. Vladimir's Seminary Press, 1985.

Healey, John B. *Charismatic Renewal: Reflections of a Pastor*. New York: Paulist Press, 1976.

Heyer, Robert, ed. *Pentecostal Catholics*. New York: Paulist Press, 1974.

Heyrman, Christine Leigh. *Southern Cross: The Beginnings of the Bible Belt*. New York: Alfred Knopf, 1997.

Hitchcock, James, and Gloriana Bednarski. *Catholic Perspectives: Charismatic*. Chicago: Thomas Moore Press, 1980.

Hopko, Thomas. *The Fullness of God: Essays on Orthodoxy, Ecumenism and Modern Society*. Crestwood, NY: St. Vladimir's Press, 1982.

———. *Bible and Church History*, Vol. II of *The Orthodox Church: An Elementary Handbook on the Orthodox Church*. New York: The Department of Religious Education, The Orthodox Church in America, 1976.

———. *Doctrine*, Vol. I of *The Orthodox Church: An Elementary Handbook on the Orthodox Church*. New York: The Department of

Religious Education, The Orthodox Church in America, 1976.

————. *The Spirit of God.* Wilton, CT: Morehouse-Barlow, 1976.

————. *Spirituality.* Vol. IV of *The Orthodox Church: An Elementary Handbook on the Orthodox Church.* New York: The Department of Religious Education, The Orthodox Church in America, 1976.

————. ed. *Women and the Priesthood.* Crestwood, NY: St. Vladimir's Press, 1992.

————. *Worship.* Vol. II of *The Orthodox Church: An Elementary Handbook on the Orthodox Church.* New York: The Department of Religious Education, The Orthodox Church in America, 1976.

Hollenweger, Walter. *The Pentecostals: The Charismatic Movement in the Churches.* Minneapolis, MN: Fortress Press, 1972.

Hoekema, Anthony A. *Tongues and Spirit-Baptism: A Biblical and Theological Evaluation.* Grand Rapids, MI: Baker Book House, 1981.

Hovenden, Gerald. *Speaking in Tongues: The New Testament Evidence in Context.* Sheffield, England: Sheffield Academic Press, 2002.

Hummel, Charles. *Fire in the Fireplace,* Downers Grove, IL: InterVarsity Press, 1994.

Humphrey, Edith M. *Ecstasy and Intimacy: When the Holy Spirit Meets the Human Spirit.* Grand Rapids, MI: Eerdmans, 2006.

Hunt, Stephen, Malcolm Hamilton, and Tony Walter, eds. *Charismatic Christianity: Sociological Perspectives.* New York: St. Martin's Press, 1997.

Jacobson, Douglas. *Thinking in the Spirit: Theologies of the Early Pentecostal Movement.* Bloomington, IN: Indiana University Press, 2003.

Johns, Cheryl Bridges. *Pentecostal Formation: A Pedagogy Among the Oppressed.* Sheffield, England: Sheffield Academic Press, 1993.

Johnson, Luke Timothy. *Religious Experience in Earliest Christianity.* Minneapolis, MN: Fortress Press, 1998.

Jones, Charles Edwin. *The Charismatic Movement: A Guide to the Study of Neo-Pentecostalism With Emphasis on Anglo-American Sources.* 2 vols. Metuchen, NJ: American Theological Library Association and Scarecrow Press, 1995.

Jungman, Josef A. *The Early Liturgy: To the Time of Gregory the Great.* Translated by Francis Brunner. Notre Dame, IN: University of Notre Dame Press, 1959.

Kärkkäinen, Veli-Matti. *One With God: Salvation as Deification and Justification.* Collegeville, MN: Liturgical Press, 2004.

Karmiris, John. *The Status and Ministry of the Laity in the Orthodox Church.* Brookline, MA: Holy Cross Orthodox Press, 1994.

Kay, William K. and Anne E. Dyer. *Pentecostal and Charismatic Studies.* London: SCM Press, 2004.

Kelsey, Morton. *Tongues Speaking: The History and Meaning of Charismatic Experience.* New York: Crossroads Publishing, 1981.

Kelso, Scott. *Ice on Fire: A New Day for the 21st Century Church.* Nashville: Nelson Books, 2006.

Kerr, John Stevens. *The Fire Flares Anew: A Look at the New Pentecostalism.* Philadelphia: Fortress Press, 1974.

King, Joseph Hilary. *From Passover to Pentecost.* Franklin Springs, GA: Advocate Press, 1976.

Kizhakkeparampil, Isaac. *The Invocation of the Holy Spirit as Constitutive of the Sacraments According to Cardinal Yves Congar.* Rome: Gregorian University Press, 1995.

Krestiankin, John. *May God Grant You Wisdom! The Letters of Fr. John Krestiankin.* Wildwood, CA: St. Xenia Skete, 2007.

Krivocheine, Basil. *In the Light of Christ.* Crestwood, NY: St. Vladimir's Seminary Press, 1986.

Küng, Hans. *The Church.* Garden City, NY: Image Books, 1976.

———. *Infallible?* London: William Collins, 1977.

LaBerge, Agnes N. O. *What God Hath Wrought.* Chicago: Herald Publishing Co., n.d. Reprint, New York: Garland Publishing, 1985.

Land, Stephan J. *Pentecostal Spirituality.* Sheffield, England: Sheffield Academic Press, 2001.

Laurentin, René. *Catholic Pentecostalism: An In-depth Report on the*

Charismatic Renewal by a Renowned International Theologian. Garden City, NY: Doubleday, 1977.

Lawler, Mary. *Marcus Garvey: Black Nationalist Leader.* New York: Chelsea House, 1988.

Lederle, H. I. *Treasures Old and New.* Peabody, MA: Hendrickson Publishers, 1988.

Lesser, R. H. *The Holy Spirit and Charismatic Renewal.* Bangalore: Asian Trading Corporation, 1996.

Lim, David. *Spiritual Gifts: A Fresh Look.* Springfield, MO: Gospel Publishing House, 1998.

Limouris, Gennadios, ed. *Come, Holy Spirit: Renew the Whole Creation.* Brookline, MA: Holy Cross Orthodox Press, 1991.

Livadeas, Themistocles. *The Real Truth Concerning Apostolos Makrakis.* Translated by D. Cummings. Chicago: The Orthodox Christian Educational Society, 1952.

MacArthur, John. *Charismatic Chaos.* Grand Rapids, MI: Zondervan, 1992.

———. *The Charismatics: A Doctrinal Perspective.* Grand Rapids, MI: Zondervan, 1978.

Macchia, Frank D. *Baptized in the Holy Spirit.* Grand Rapids, MI: Zondervan, 2006.

Mackey, J. P. *The Modern Meaning of Tradition.* New York: Herder & Herder, 1963.

MacNutt, Francis. *Healing.* Notre Dame, IN: Ave Maria Press, 1974.

———. *The Nearly Perfect Crime: How the Church Almost Killed the Ministry of Healing.* Grand Rapids, MI: Chosen, 2005.

———. *Overcome by the Spirit.* Tarrytown, NY: Fleming H. Revell, 1990.

Mahan, Asa. *Baptism of the Holy Spirit.* Clinton, NY: Williams Publishers, n.d.

Makrakis, Apostolos. *The Political Philosophy of the Orthodox Church.* Translated by D. Cummings. Chicago: The Orthodox Christian Educational Society, 1965.

Maloney, George. *The Breath of the Mystic.* Denville, NJ: Dimension Books, 1974.

———. *Invaded by God: Mysticism and the Indwelling Trinity.* Denville, NJ: Dimension Books, 1979.

———. *The Jesus Prayer.* Pecos, NM: Dove Publications, 1974.

———. *Jesus, Set Me Free!* Denville, NJ: Dimension Books, 1977.

———. *Listen, Prophets!* Denville, NJ: Dimension Books, n.d.

———. *Mystic of Fire and Light.* Denville, NJ: Dimension Books, 1975.

———. *Prayer of the Heart.* Notre Dame, IN: Ave Maria Press, 1981.

———. *Uncreated Energy: A Journey Into the Authentic Sources of Christian Faith.* Amity, NY: Amity House, 1987.

Malony, H. Newton, and A. Adams Lovekin. *Glossolalia: Behavioral Science Perspectives on Speaking in Tongues.* Oxford: Oxford University Press, 1985.

Mansfield, M. Robert. *Spirit & Gospel in Mark.* Peabody, MA: Hendrickson, 1987.

Mansfield, Patti Gallagher. *As by a New Pentecost: The Dramatic Beginning of the Charismatic Catholic Renewal.* Steubenville, OH: Franciscan University Press, 1992.

Mantzaridis, Georgios I. *The Deification of Man.* Crestwood, NY: St. Vladimir's Seminary Press, 1984.

Marshall, Catherine. *The Helper.* Waco, TX: Chosen Books, 1978.

Martin, David, and Peter Mullen, ed. *Strange Gifts: A Guide to Charismatic Renewal.* Oxford: Basil Blackwell, 1984.

Martin, George, ed. *Scripture and the Charismatic Renewal.* Ann Arbor, MI: Servant, 1979.

Martin, Ralph. *Fire on the Earth: What God Is Doing in the World Today.* Ann Arbor, MI: 1975.

———. comp. *New Wine, New Skins.* New York: Paulist Press, 1976.

———. *Unless the Lord Build the House: The Church and the New Pentecost.* Notre Dame, IN: Ave Maria Press, 1971.

Matthews, David, L. *The Perfecting of the Saints: How Pentecostal Terminology Is Bewitching the Charismatic Movement*. Malta, OH: Sozo Ministries, 1977.

Mazza, Enrico. *Mystagogy: A Theology of Liturgy in the Patristic Age*. Translated by Matthew J. O'Connell. New York: Pueblo Publishing, 1989.

McCarthy, Timothy G. *The Catholic Tradition: Before and After Vatican II, 1878–1993*. Chicago: Loyola University Press, 1994.

McDonnell, Kilian. *Catholic Pentecostalism: Problems in Evaluation*. Pecos, NM: Dove Publications, 1970.

———. *The Charismatic Movement in the Churches*. New York: Seabury Press, 1976.

———, ed. *The Holy Spirit and Power: The Catholic Charismatic Renewal*. New York: Doubleday, 1975.

———. *The Other Hand of God: The Holy Spirit as the Universal Touch and Goal*. Collegeville, MN: Liturgical Press, 2003.

———. *Toward a New Pentecost for a New Evangelization*. Collegeville, MN: Liturgical Press, 1993.

——— and Arnold Bittlinger, *The Baptism of the Holy Spirit as an Ecumenical Problem*. Ann Arbor, MI: Word of Life, 1972.

———, and George T. Montague, *Christian Initiation and Baptism in the Holy Spirit*. Collegeville, MN: The Liturgical Press, 1991.

McGee, Gary B. *People of the Spirit: The Assemblies of God*. Springfield, MO: Gospel Publishing House, 2004.

McIntire, C. T., ed. *God, History and Historians*. New York: Oxford Press, 1977. 50.

McManners, John, ed. *The Oxford Illustrated History of Christianity*. Oxford: Oxford University Press, 1990.

Meyendorff, John. *Byzantine Theology*. New York: Fordham Press, 1979.

———. *Imperial Unity and Christian Divisions: The Church 450–680 A.D.* Crestwood, NY: St. Vladimir's Seminary Press, 1989.

———. *The Primacy of Peter*. Crestwood, NY: St. Vladimir's Seminary

Press, 1992.

————*St. Gregory Palamas and Orthodox Spirituality.* Crestwood, NY: St. Vladimir's Seminary Press, 1974.

Meyendorff, Paul. *The Anointing of the Sick.* Crestwood, NY: St. Vladimir's Seminary Press, 2009.

Middleton, Herman A. *Precious Vessels of the Holy Spirit: The Lives & Counsels of Contemporary Elders of Greece.* Thessalonika, Greece: Protecting Veil Press, 2003.

Miller, Donald E., and Tetsunao Ymamori. *Global Pentecostalism: The New Face of Christian Social Engagement.* Berkeley, CA: University of California Press, 2007.

Minns, Denis. *Irenaeus.* London: Geoffrey Chapman, 1994.

Mitilinaios, Athanasios. *Homilies on the Book of Revelation, Volume 1.* Translated by Constantine Zalalas. Bethlehem, PA: St. Nicodemos Publications, 2009.

Montague, George. *The Holy Spirit: Growth of a Biblical Tradition.* New York: Paulist Press, 1976.

————. *The Spirit and His Gifts.* New York: Paulist Press, 1974.

Moore, David. *The Shepherding Movement.* London: T & T Clark, 2003.

Moran, Gabriel. *Scripture and Tradition: A Survey of the Controversy.* New York: Herder & Herder, 1963.

Morelli, George. *Healing: Orthodox Christianity and Scientific Psychology.* Fairfax, VA: Eastern Christian Publications, 2006.

Morfessis, Anthony. *God Made Me for His Plans.* Johnstown, PA: Shepherd Publishing, 1980.

Morgan-Wynne, John Eifion. *Holy Spirit and Religious Experience in Christian Literature ca. AD 90–200.* Milton Keynes, England: Paternoster Press, 2006.

Moriarty, Michael G. *The New Charismatic: A Concerned Voice Responds to Dangerous New Trends,* Grand Rapids, MI: Zondervan, 1992.

Morris, John Warren. *The Charismatic Movement: An Orthodox Evalu-*

ation. Brookline, MA: Holy Cross Orthodox Press, 1984.

Moser, Maureen Beyer. *Teacher of Holiness: The Holy Spirit in Origen's Commentary on the Epistle to the Romans.* Piscataway, NJ: Gorgias Press, 2005.

Mühlen, Heribert. *Charismatic Theology: Initiation in the Spirit.* New York: Paulist Press, 1978.

Needham, N. R. *2000 Years of Christ's Power Part One: The Age of the Early Church Fathers.* London: Grace Publications Trust, 1997.

Neitz, Mary Jo. *Charisma and Community: A Study of Religious Commitment With the Charismatic Renewal.* New Brunswick, NJ: Transaction Books, 1987.

Nellas, Panayiotos. *Deification in Christ: The Nature of the Human Person.* Crestwood, NY: St. Vladimir's Seminary Press, 1987.

Nicozisin, George. *The Hope of the Hopeless, the Savior of the Tempest-Tossed: Sermons by Father George Nicozisin.* N.p., 1985.

Noll, Mark. *The Rise of Evangelicalism: The Age of Edwards, Whitefield and the Wesleys.* Downers Grove, IL: InterVarsity Press, 2003.

Nuns of the Holy Cenobitic Monastery of Panaghia Eleousa. *Our Geronda. The Life and Miracles of the Late Elder of Patmos, Amphilochios Makris.* Translated by Christodoulos G. Papadeas, Margaret H. Georgiadis, and Margarita Dolley. Rotso, Kalymnos, Greece: Holy Cenobitic Women's Monastery of Panaghia Eleousa, 1995.

O'Connor, Edward D. *Pope Paul and the Spirit: Charisms and Church Renewal in the Teaching of Paul IV.* Notre Dame, IN: Ave Maria Press, 1978.

Oden, Thomas, ed. *Phoebe Palmer: Selected Writings.* New York: Paulist Press, 1988.

Oh, Gwang Seok, *John Wesley's Ecclesiology :A Study in Its Sources and Development.* Lanham, MD: Scarecrow Press, 2008.

Okholm, Dennis. *Monk Habits for Everyday People.* Grand Rapids, MI: Brazos Press, 2007.

Oleksa, Michael, ed. *Alaskan Missionary Spirituality.* New York: Paulist

Press, 1987.

Orsini, Joseph. *The Cost in Pentecost*. Plainfield, NJ: Logos International, 1977.

Osborn, Eric. *Irenaeus of Lyons*. Cambridge, England: Cambridge University Press, 2001.

Paisios, Elder. *Spiritual Awakening*. Vol. 2 of *Elder Paisios of Mount Athos Spiritual Counsels*. Translated by Peter Chamberas. Souroti, Thessaloniki, Greece: Holy Monastery of Evangelist John the Theologian, 2008.

———. *With Pain and Love for Contemporary Man*. Vol. 1 of *Elder Paisios of Mount Athos Spiritual Counsels*. Translated by Cornelia Tsakiridou and Maria Spanou. Souroti, Thessaloniki, Greece: Holy Monastery of Evangelist John the Theologian, 2007.

Palma, Anthony D. *The Holy Spirit: A Pentecostal Perspective*. Springfield, MO: Logion Press, 2001.

Papacostas, Seraphim. *Repentance*. Athens, Greece: The Zoe Brotherhood of Theologians, 1958.

Papadopoulos, Stylianos. *The Garden of the Holy Spirit: Elder Iakovos of Evia*. Clearwater, FL: Orthodox Witness, 2007.

Patterson, Eric, and Edmund Rybarczyk. *The Future of Pentecostalism in the United States*. Lanham, MD: Rowan & Littlefield, 2007.

Pelikan, Jaroslav. *The Emergence of the Catholic Tradition 100–600*. Vol. 1 of *The Christian Tradition: A History of the Development of Doctrine*. Chicago: University of Chicago Press, 1971.

———. *The Spirit of Eastern Christendom 600–1700*. Vol. 2 of *The Christian Tradition: A History of the Development of Doctrine*. Chicago: University of Chicago Press, 1974.

Peters, John Leland. *Christian Perfection and American Methodism*. Grand Rapids, MI: Francis Asbury Press, 1985.

Poloma, Margaret M. *The Charismatic Movement: Is There a New Pentecost?* Boston: Twayne Publishers, 1982.

Prange, Erwin E. *The Gift Is Already Yours*. Plainfield, NJ: Logos

International, 1973. Prepared by the Theological-Historical Commission for the Great Jubilee of the Year 2000. *The Holy Spirit, Lord and Giver of Life.* New York: Crossroad Publishing, 1997.

Porphyrios, Elder. *Wounded by Love: The Life and Wisdom of Elder Porphyrios.* Translated by John Raffan. Limni, Evia, Greece: Denise Harvey, 2005.

Protopopov, Michael A. *A Russian Presence: A History of the Russian Orthodox Church in Australia.* Piscataway, NJ: Gorgias Press, 2006.

Purves, Jim. *The Triune God and the Charismatic Movement.* Milton Keynes, England: Paternoster Press, 2004.

Quebedeaux, Richard. *The New Charismatics: The Origins, Development and Significance of Neo-Pentecostalism.* Garden City, NY: Doubleday, 1976.

———. *The New Charismatics II: How a Christian Renewal Movement Became Part of the American Religious Mainstream.* New York: Harper & Row, 1983.

Raboteau, Albert. *Slave Religion: The "Invisible Institution" in the Antebellum South.* New York: Oxford University Press, 2004.

———. *A Sorrowful Joy: The Spiritual Journey of an African-American Man in Late Twentieth-Century America.* New York: Paulist Press, 2002.

Rahner, Karl. *Most Recent Writing,* Vol. IV of *Theological Investigations.* Translated by Kevin Smyth. New York: The Seabury Press, 1974.

Ranaghan, Kevin. *Catholic Pentecostals.* New York: Paulist Press, 1969.

———. *The Spirit in the Church.* New York: Seabury Press, 1979.

Ratzinger, Joseph. *Called to Communion: Understanding the Church Today.* San Francisco: Ignatius Press, 1996.

Rea, John. *The Layman's Commentary on the Holy Spirit.* Plainfield, NJ: Logos International, 1972.

Riggs, Ralph. *The Spirit Himself.* Springfield, MO: Gospel Publishing House, 1949.

Robeck Jr., Cecil M. *The Azusa Street Mission and Revival.* Nashville:

Thomas Nelson, 2006.

———. *Charismatic Experiences in History.* Peabody, MA: Hendrickson, 1985.

Roberson, Dave. *The Walk of the Spirit—The Walk of Power: The Vital Role of Praying in Tongues.* Tulsa, OK: Dave Roberson Ministries, 1999.

Roberts, Oral. *The Baptism of the Holy Spirit and the Value of Speaking in Tongues Today.* Tulsa, OK: Oral Roberts Evangelistic Association, 1964.

Rogers Jr., Eugene F. *After the Spirit: A Constructive Pneumatology From Resources Outside the Modern West.* Grand Rapids, MI: Eerdmans, 2005.

Rose, Seraphim. *Orthodoxy and the Religion of the Future.* Platina, CA: St. Herman of Alaska Brotherhood, 1975.

Runyan, Theodore, ed. *What the Spirit Is Saying to the Churches.* New York: Hawthorn Books, 1975.

Ruthven, John. *On the Cessation of the Charismata: The Protestant Polemic on Post-Biblical Miracles.* Sheffield, England: Sheffield Academic Press, 1993.

Ryan, John J. *The Jesus People.* Chicago: Life in Christ, 1970.

Rybarczyk, Edmund. *Beyond Salvation: Eastern Orthodoxy and Classical Pentecostalism on Becoming Like Christ.* Milton Keynes, England: Paternoster, 2004.

Sandage, Jerry, ed. *Roman Catholic/Pentecostal Dialogue (1977–1982): A Study in Developing Ecumenism.* Frankfurt am Main, Germany: Verlag Peter Lang, 1987.

Satyavrata, Ivan. *The Holy Spirit: Lord and Life-Giver.* Downers Grove, IL: IVP Academic, 2009.

Schmemann, Alexander. *The Eucharist: The Sacrament of the Kingdom.* Translated by Paul Kachur. Crestwood, NY: St. Vladimir's Seminary Press, 1988.

———. *For the Life of the World.* Crestwood, NY: St. Vladimir's Seminary Press, 1973.

———. *Introduction to Liturgical Theology.* Crestwood, NY: St. Vladimir's Seminary Press, 1986.

Schultz, Hans-Joachim. *The Byzantine Liturgy: Symbolic Structure and Faith Expression.* Translated Matthew J. O'Connell. New York: Pueblo Publishing, 1986.

Sherrill, John. *They Speak With Other Tongues.* Tappan, NJ: Fleming H. Revell, 1973.

Shelton, James B. *Mighty in Word and Deed: The Role of the Holy Spirit in Luke–Acts.* Peabody, MA: Hendrickson, 1991.

Shenouda III, H. H. Pope. *The Heresy of Salvation in a Moment.* Translated by Wedad Abbas. Cairo, Egypt: Coptic Orthodox Patriarchate, 1999.

Simmons, Dale H. *E. W. Kenyon and the Postbellum Pursuit of Peace, Power, and Plenty.* Lanham, MD: Scarecrow Press, 1997.

Small, Franklin. *Living Waters: A Sure Guide for Your Faith.* Winnipeg, Canada: The Columbia Press Limited, n.d.

Snyder, Howard. *The Divided Flame: Wesleyans and the Charismatic Renewal.* Grand Rapids, MI: Francis Asbury Press, 1986.

Spittler, Russell P., ed. *Perspectives on the New Pentecostalism* Grand Rapids, MI: Baker Book House, 1976.

Stagg, Frank., E. Glenn Hinson, Wayne E. Oates. *Glossolalia: Tongue Speaking in Biblical, Historical, and Psychological Perspective.* Nashville: Abingdon Press, 1967.

Staniloae, Dumitru. *Tradition and Modernity in Theology.* Iasi, Romania: Center for Romanian Studies, 2002.

Stephanou, Eusebius. *Belief and Practice in the Orthodox Church.*

———. *Charisma and Gnosis in Orthodox Thought.* Fort Wayne, IN: Logos Ministry, 1975.

———. *The Charismata in the Early Church Fathers.* Destin, FL: St. Symeon the New Theologian Orthodox Brotherhood, n.d.

———. *Chrismation, the Hidden Sacrament.* Destin, FL: N.p., 1988.

———. ed. and trans. *Exorcism—Prayers of Deliverance.* Fort Wayne, IN: Logos Foundation for Orthodox Awakening, 1974.

———. *A Manual on the Basic Principles of Orthodox Renewal.* Destin, FL: St. Symeon the New Theologian Press, 2008.

———. *Renewal Pains in the Orthodox Church.* Fort Wayne, IN: Logos Ministry, 1982.

———. *Sacramentalized but Not Evangelized.* Destin, FL: St. Symeon the New Theologian Press, 2005.

———. *Sounding the Trumpet in the Orthodox Church.* Destin, FL: St. Symeon the New Theologian Press, 2005.

Stephens, Rand J. *The Fire Spreads: Holiness and Pentecostalism in the American South.* Cambridge, MA: Harvard University Press, 2008.

Stethatos, Maria. *The Voice of a Priest Crying in the Wilderness.* El Cajon, CA: CSN Books, 2008.

Stibbe, Mark. *Times of Refreshing: A Practical Theology of Revival for Today.* London: Marshall Pickering, 1995.

Stiles, J. E. *The Gift of the Holy Spirit.* Old Tappan, NJ: Fleming H. Revell, 1971.

Stoeffler, F. Earnest, ed. *Continental Pietism and Early American Christianity.* Grand Rapids, MI: Eerdmans, 1976.

Stott, John R. W. *Baptism and Fullness: The Work of the Holy Spirit Today.* Downers Grove, IL: InterVarsity Press, 1976.

Stronstad, Roger. *The Charismatic Theology of St. Luke.* Peabody, MA: Hendrickson, 1984.

Stylianopoulos, Theodore. *Christ Is in our Midst: Spiritual Renewal in the Orthodox Church.* Brookline, MA: Greek Orthodox Archdiocese Department of Religious Education, 1981.

———. *The Good News of Christ.* Brookline, MA: Holy Cross Orthodox Press, 1991.

———. *The Way of Christ: Gospel, Spiritual Life and Renewal in Orthodoxy.* Brookline, MA: Holy Cross Orthodox Press, 2002.

Sumrall, Lester. *The Gifts and Ministries of the Holy Spirit.* New Kensington, PA; Whitaker House, 2003.

Suenens, Leon J. Cardinal. *Ecumenism and Charismatic Renewal: Theological and Pastoral Orientations.* Ann Arbor, MI: Servant Books, 1978.

———. *A New Pentecost?* Translated by Francis Martin. New York: Seabury Press, 1975.

———, and Dom Helder Camara. *Charismatic Renewal and Social Action: A Dialogue.* Ann Arbor, MI: Servant Books, 1979.

Sullivan, Francis. A. *Charisms and Charismatic Renewal: A Biblical and Theological Study.* Ann Arbor: MI: Servant, 1982.

Suurmond, Jean-Jacques. *Word and Spirit at Play: Towards a Charismatic Theology.* Grand Rapids, MI: Eerdmans, 1994.

Swete, Henry Barclay. *The Holy Spirit in the Ancient Church.* Grand Rapids, MI: Baker Book House, 1966.

———. *The Holy Spirit in the New Testament.* Grand Rapids, MI: Baker Books, 1964.

Synan, Vinson, ed. *Aspects of Pentecostal-Charismatic Origins.* Plainfield, NJ: Logos International, 1975.

———. *The Century of the Holy Spirit.* Nashville: Thomas Nelson Publishers, 2001.

———. *Charismatic Bridges.* Ann Arbor, MI: Word of Life, 1974.

———. *The Holiness-Pentecostal Movement in the United States.* Grand Rapids, MI: Eerdmans, 1971.

———. *In the Latter Days: The Outpouring of the Holy Spirit in the Twentieth Century.* Ann Arbor, MI; Servant Books, 1984.

———, and Ralph Rath. *Launching the Decade of Evangelism.* South Bend, IN: North American Renewal Service Committee, 1990.

———. *The Old-Time Power: A History of the Pentecostal Holiness Church.* Franklin Springs, GA: Advocate Press, 1973.

———. *The Twentieth-Century Pentecostal Explosion.* Altamonte Springs, FL: Creation House, 1987.

———. *Under His Banner: History of Full Gospel Business Men's Fel-

lowship International. Costa Mesa, CA: Gift Publications, 1992.

Tarasar, Constance J., ed. *Orthodox America 1794–1976: Development of the Orthodox Church in America*. Syosset, NY: The Orthodox Church in America Department of History and Archives, 1975.

Terry-Thompson, A. C. *The History of the African Orthodox Church*. New York: N.p., 1956.

Thomas, Stephen. *Deification in the Eastern Orthodox Tradition: A Biblical Perspective*. Piscataway, NJ: Gorgias Press, 2007.

Tomlinson, A. J. *Sanctification, a Peculiar Treasure*. Cleveland, TN: Committee on Doctrine, The Church of God of Prophecy, n.d.

Torrance, Thomas F. *Theology in Reconciliation: Essays Towards Evangelical and Catholic Unity in East and West*. Grand Rapids, MI: Eerdmans, 1975.

Trader, Alexis. *In Peace Let Us Pray to the Lord: An Orthodox Interpretation of the Gifts of the Spirit*. Salisbury, MA: Regina Orthodox Press, 2002.

Trifa, Valerian D. *Holy Sacraments for Orthodox Christians*. Jackson, MI: The Romanian Episcopate of America, n.d.

Tsirpanlis, Constantine. *Introduction to Eastern Patristic Thought and Orthodox Theology*. Collegeville, MN: Liturgical Press, 1991.

Tuttle Jr., Robert G. *Mysticism in the Wesleyan Tradition*. Grand Rapids, MI: Francis Asbury Press, 1989.

Tugwell, Simon, George Every, Peter Hocken, and John Orme Mills. *New Heaven? New Earth? An Encounter With Pentecostalism*. Springfield, IL: Templegate, 1977.

Turner, Max. *The Holy Spirit and Spiritual Gifts*. Peabody, MA: Hendrickson, 1996.

Urshan, Andrew. *The Life of Andrew Bar David Urshan*. Stockton, CA: Apostolic Press, 1967.

Vagaggini, Cyprian. *Theological Dimensions of the Liturgy: A General Treatise on the Theology of the Liturgy*. Translated by Leonard J. Doyle and W. A. Jurgens. Collegeville, MN: Liturgical Press, 1976.

Vicher, Lukas, ed. *Spirit of God, Spirit of Christ: Ecumenical Reflections on the Filoque Controversy.* London: SPCK, 1981.

Vlachos, Hierotheos. *The Illness and Cure of the Soul in the Orthodox Tradition.* Translated by Effie Mavromichali. Levadia, Greece: Birth of the Theotokos Monastery, 1993.

———. *Orthodox Psychotherapy.* Translated by Effie Mavromichali. Levadia, Greece: Birth of the Theotokos Monastery, 1994.

———. *Orthodox Spirituality, a Brief Introduction.* Translated by Effie Mavromichali. Levadia, Greece: Birth of the Theotokos Monastery, 1993.

Volf, Miroslav. *After Our Likeness: The Church as the Image of the Trinity.* Grand Rapids, MI: Eerdmans, 1998.

Von Campenhausen, Hans. *Ecclesiastical Authority and Spiritual Power in the Church of the First Three Centuries.* Peabody, MA: Hendrickson, 1997.

Wagner, C. Peter. *The Third Wave of the Holy Spirit: Encountering the Power of Signs and Wonders.* Ann Arbor, MI: Vine Books, 1988.

Ware, Kallistos. *The Power of the Name: The Jesus Prayer in Orthodox Spirituality.* Oxford: SLG Press, 1974.

Winslow, Jack C. *Christa Seva Sangha*, Westminster, England: Society for the Propagation of the Gospel in Foreign Parts, 1930.

Wakefield, Gavin. *Alexander Boddy, Pentecostal Anglican Pioneer.* Milton Keynes, England: Paternoster Press, 2007.

Walker, Andrew, and Costa Carras, eds. *Living Orthodoxy in the Modern World.* London: SPCK, 1996.

Walston, Rick. *The Speaking in Tongues Controversy.* Eugene, OR: Wipf & Stock, 2003.

Ware, Timothy. *The Orthodox Church.* New York: Penguin Books, 1980.

Wegman, Herman. *Christian Worship in East and West: A Study Guide in Liturgical History.* Translated by Gordon W. Lathrop. New York: Pueblo Publishing, 1985.

Welker, Michael, ed. *The Work of the Spirit: Pneumatology and Pente-

costalism. Grand Rapids, MI: Eerdmans, 2006.

Wesley, John. *A Plain Account of Christian Perfection*. Cincinnati: Methodist Book Concern, 1925.

———. *The Letters of Rev. John Wesley*. Edited by John Telford. 8 vols. London: Epsworth Press, 1931.

Westerlund, David. *Global Pentecostalism: Encounter With Other Religious Traditions*. London: I. B. Tauris, 2009.

Wild, Robert. *Enthusiasm in the Spirit.* Notre Dame, IN: Ave Maria Press, 1975.

Wilgen, Ralph M. *The Rhine Flows Into the Tiber: A History of Vatican II*. Rockford, IL: TAN Books, 1985.

Wilkerson, David, with Elizabeth Sherrill and John Sherrill. *The Cross and the Switchblade*. New York: Random House, 1963.

Wilkinson, Michael, ed. *Canadian Pentecostalism: Transition and Transformation.* Montreal: McGill-Queen's University Press, 2009.

Williams, J. Rodman. *The Era of the Spirit.* Plainfield, NJ: Logos International, 1971.

———. *The Gift of the Holy Spirit Today.* Plainfield, NJ: Logos International, 1980.

———. *The Pentecostal Reality.* Plainfield, NJ: Logos International, 1972.

Wilson, Mark W., ed. *Spirit and Renewal: Essays in Honor of J. Rodman Williams.* Sheffield, England: Sheffield Academic Press.

Wood, Laurence. *The Meaning of Pentecost in Early Methodism: Rediscovering John Fletcher as John Wesley's Vindicator and Designated Successor.* Lanham, MD: Scarecrow Press, 2002.

Word of God. *The Life in the Spirit Seminars Team Manual (Catholic Edition).* Ann Arbor: Servant Books, 1979.

Yannaras, Christos. *The Freedom of Morality.* Crestwood, NY: St. Vladimir's Seminary Press, 1996.

Yong, Amos. *The Spirit Poured Out on All Flesh: Pentecostalism and the Possibility of Global Theology.* Grand Rapids, MI: Baker Academic, 2005.

Yeide, Harry. *Studies in Classical Pietism: The Flowering of the Ecclesiola.* New York: Peter Lang, 1997.

Zacharias, Archimandrite. *The Hidden Man of the Heart (1 Peter 3:4): The Cultivation of the Heart in Orthodox Christian Anthropology.* Waymart, PA: Mount Thabor Publishing, 2008.

Zervakos, Philotheos. *Autobiography, Homilies and Miracles.* Translated by Nicholas Palis, Joseph, and Despina Chaffee. Thessaloniki, Greece: Orthodox Kypseli Publications, 2006.

Zizioulos, John. *Being as Communion.* Crestwood, NY: St. Vladimir's Seminary Press, 1985.

Zodhiates, Spiros. *Tongues.* Ridgefield, NJ: AMG Press, 1974.

Dissertations

Catanello, Ignatius A., "The Effects of the Charismatic Movement on Local Ecumenism: Descriptive Research." PhD diss., New York University, 1983.

Cremeens, Timothy. "The Pentecostal-Charismatic Movement: An Introduction for Orthodox Christians." MDiv diss., St. Vladimir's Orthodox Theological Seminary, 1993.

Engelsviken, Tormod. "The Gift of the Spirit: An Analysis and Evaluation of the Charismatic Movement from a Lutheran Theological Perspective." PhD diss., Aquinas Institute of Theology, 1981.

Farkas, Thomas George. "William H. Durham and the Sanctification Controversy in Early American Pentecostalism." PhD diss., Southwestern Baptist Theological Seminary, 1993.

Lie, Geir. "E. W. Kenyon: Cult Founder or Evangelical Minster: An Historical Analysis of Kenyon's Theology With Particular Emphasis on the Roots and Influences." Master's diss., Norwegian Lutheran School of Theology, 1994.

Waldvogel, Edith Lydia. "The 'Overcoming Life': A Study in the Reformed Evangelical Origins of Pentecostalism." PhD diss., Harvard University, 1977.

Wheelock, Donald Ray. "Spirit Baptism in American Pentecostal Thought." PhD diss., Emory University Graduate School, 1983.

Journal Articles and Book Chapters

Chakos, John. "The Charismatic Revival and Its Implications for Orthodoxy." *Concern*, X, no. 3 (Fall 1975): 6–9.

Dabney, Lyle. "Saul's Armor: The Problem and the Promise of Pentecostal Theology Today," *Pneuma: The Journal of the Society for Pentecostal Studies*, 23, no. 1 (Spring 2001): 115–46.

Emmert, Athanasius. "Come, Holy Spirit!" *The Logos*, 5, no. 3 (March 1972): 8–9.

———. "The Glory Is His Alone." *The Logos*, 5, no. 6 (June–July 1972): 8–9.

———. "Making the Power of the Holy Spirit Our Own: The Wonderful Promise of God." *The Logos*, 5, no. 2 (February 1972): 8–9.

———. "The Pentecostal Power Inherent in the Orthodox Church." *The Logos*, 5, no. 4 (April 1972): 8–10.

———. "The Power of the Holy Spirit: A Need for Our Day." *The Logos*, 5, no. 1 (January 1972): 14–6.

———. "The Unfamiliar Is Threatening to Some Orthodox: Why the Charismatic Movement Is Not Foreign to Orthodoxy." *The Logos*, 5, no. 5 (May 1972): 11–13.

Frame, Randall. "UnOrthodox Behavior?" *Christianity Today*, 37, no. 18 (December 13, 1993): 57.

Hunter, Harold. "Tongues-Speech: A Patristic Analysis," *Journal of the Evangelical Theological Society*, 23, no. 2 (June 1980): 125–137.

Iakovos, Archbishop. "Exorcism and Exorcists in Orthodox Tradition," *Upbeat*, 7, no. 8 (May/June 1974): 15–19.

Johnson, Ann. "Home Pages: Prosphora," *Orthodox Outlook*, 97 (May–June 2002): 24–26.

Macchia, Frank. "Justification Through New Creation: The Holy Spirit and the Doctrine by Which the Church Stands or Falls," *Theology*

Today, 58, no. 2 (July 2001): 202–217.

———. "The Tongues of Pentecost: A Pentecostal Perspective on the Promise and Change of Pentecostal/Roman Catholic Dialogue," *Journal of Ecumenical Studies,* 35, no. 1 (Winter 1998): 1–18.

McMullen, Cary. "Holding Their Tongues: The Assemblies of God Asks Whether Its Distinctive Teaching Is Being Lost in Outreach Efforts," *Christianity Today,* 53, no. 10 (October 2009): 15–19.

Monios, Constantine M. "BEHOLD: I Make All Things New!" *The Logos,* 5, no. 3 (March 1972): 14–6.

———. "A Breath of Spiritual Fragrance." *The Logos,* 5, no. 2 (February 1972): 10–11.

———. "A Happy Priest." *The Logos,* 5, no. 5 (May 1972): 9–10.

N.a. "A Discussion With Father Khodre." *Upbeat,* 2, no. 4 & 5 (April–May 1969): 28–33.

Nassif, Bradley. "Greek Orthodox Church Tries to Muzzle a Popular Charismatic Priest." *Christianity Today.* 27, no. 18 (November 25, 1983): 53.

Nissiotis, Nikos A. "The Unity of Scripture and Tradition: An Eastern Orthodox Contribution to the Prolegomena of Hermeneutics." *The Greek Orthodox Theological Review,* XI (1965–1966): 183–208.

Plowman, Edward E. "Mission to Orthodoxy: The 'Full Gospel.'" *Christianity Today,* (April 18, 1974): 44–45.

Stroud, Marilyn. "The Hebden Mission—Our Canadian Azusa?" *Testimony,* 90, no. 5 (May 2009): 27.

Walker, Andrew. "The Orthodox Church and the Charismatic Movement." In *Strange Gifts? A Guide to the Charismatic Movement.* Edited by David Martin and Peter Mullen, 192–207. Oxford: Basil Blackwell, 1984.

———. "Thoroughly Modern: Sociological Reflections on the Charismatic Movement From the End of the Twentieth Century." In *Charismatic Christianity: Sociological Perspectives.* Edited by Stephen Hunt, Malcolm Hamilton, and Tony Walter, 17–42. New York: St. Martin's

Press, 1997.

Yong, Amos. "As the Spirit Gives Utterance: Pentecost, Intra-Christian Ecumenism and the Wider Oikoumene." *International Review of Mission*, 92, no. 366 (July 2003): 299–314.

Pamphlets

Nicozisin, George. *Born Again Christians, Charismatics, Gifts of the Holy Spirit: An Orthodox Perspective*. New York: Greek Orthodox Department of Religious Education, n.d.

———. *Speaking in Tongues an Orthodox Perspective*. New York: Greek Orthodox Department of Religious Education, n.d.

Sound and Video Recordings

Cremeens, Fr. Timothy. *St. Symeon the New Theologian*. Destin, FL, Brotherhood of St. Symeon the New Theologian, VHS, 1992.

Emmert, Fr. Athanasius. *Israel in Prophecy*. Homewood, IL: St. Nicholas Orthodox Church, two audiocassettes, n.d.

Langdon, Fr. Joseph, *How the Holy Spirit Brings Us to Christ*. OR #44, Fort Wayne, IN: Service Committee for Orthodox Spiritual Renewal, audiocassette, n.d.

Stephanou, Rev. Eusebius, *The Baptism in the Holy Spirit: An Orthodox Understanding*. M11. Fort Wayne, IN: Logos Ministry for Orthodox Renewal, audiocassette, n.d.

———. *The Holy Spirit Glorifies Jesus*. M10. Fort Wayne, IN: Logos Ministry for Orthodox Renewal, audiocassette, 1973.

Young, Fr. Alexey, *The 12-Step Program and Orthodox Spirituality*. Beaumont: TX, Antiochian Christian Orthodox Radio Network (ACORN), two audiocassettes, n.d.

Zabrodsky, Fr. Boris, *The Sacraments in the Charismatic Experience*. H10. Fort Wayne, IN: Logos Ministry for Orthodox Renewal, audiocassette, n.d.

Unpublished Papers/ Manuscripts

Cremeens, Timothy B. "St. Symeon the New Theologian: An Eastern Orthodox Model for Charismatic Spirituality." Paper presented at the annual meeting of the Society for Pentecostal Studies. Springfield, MO: November 12, 1992, 2, V. 1–29.

About *the* Author

VERNA M. LINZEY, DD, distinguished theological researcher, prolific writer, and crusade evangelist, is recognized as one of Pentecostalism's leading thinkers and writers in the field of glossolalia and spiritual gifts. Her ministry over the past seventy years has taken her across the United States and to Haiti, India, the Philippines, Hong Kong, Europe, Mexico, and Canada.

Now ninety-five years old Dr. Linzey was influenced by some who attended or were impacted by the Azusa Street Revival, such as Ernest S. Williams and P. C. Nelson. She ministered at the Azusa Street Mission site and the Bonnie Brae Street House, where revival broke out under her ministry in December 2012.

A contributor to the Pentecostal movement, she became a minister with the Assemblies of God in 1945. Dr. Linzey wrote *The Baptism With the Holy Spirit* (foreword by Russell P. Spittler), which has been used in one hundred Bible schools in the Far East and earned her the Best Non-Fiction of the Year Award in 2006 from the San Diego Christian Writers' Guild. She also wrote *Spirit Baptism: Understanding Pentecostal Theology* (foreword by Wonsuk Ma) and is a coeditor of *Baptism in the Spirit* by her late husband Stanford E. Linzey Jr. (foreword by Stanley M. Horton).

Dr. Linzey is also a recording artist. She is author of the hymn "Oh Blessed Jesus," which is recorded on a CD by the same name. In 2010 she portrayed the lead juror in the major feature film *Iniquity*, which is based on the story of David and Bathsheba. Her song "The Rose" is featured on the soundtrack for the movie, which was sponsored in part by the Military Bible Association, an organization Dr. Linzey cofounded.

Dr. Linzey matriculated at PC Nelson's Southwest Bible School, audited the Doctor of Ministry program at Fuller Theological Seminary, and received a Doctor of Divinity degree from Kingsway Theological Seminary. She serves with distinction on the advisory boards of St. Elias Seminary and Graduate School (in the Orthodox tradition and based in the United States), Nehemiah Theological Seminary (a Pentecostal seminary based in India), and Verna Linzey Child Care Ministry, International (an Assemblies of God organization based in the Philippines).

Various media have interviewed Dr. Linzey, including KPBS, God's Learning Channel, Hosanna Broadcasting Network, and His Television Network. She is the host of *The Holy Spirit Today* radio and television broadcasts. Dr. Linzey also is listed in *Who's Who in America*, *Who's Who in the World*, and *Who's Who Among American Women*.

EMPOWERED
TO RADICALLY CHANGE
YOUR WORLD